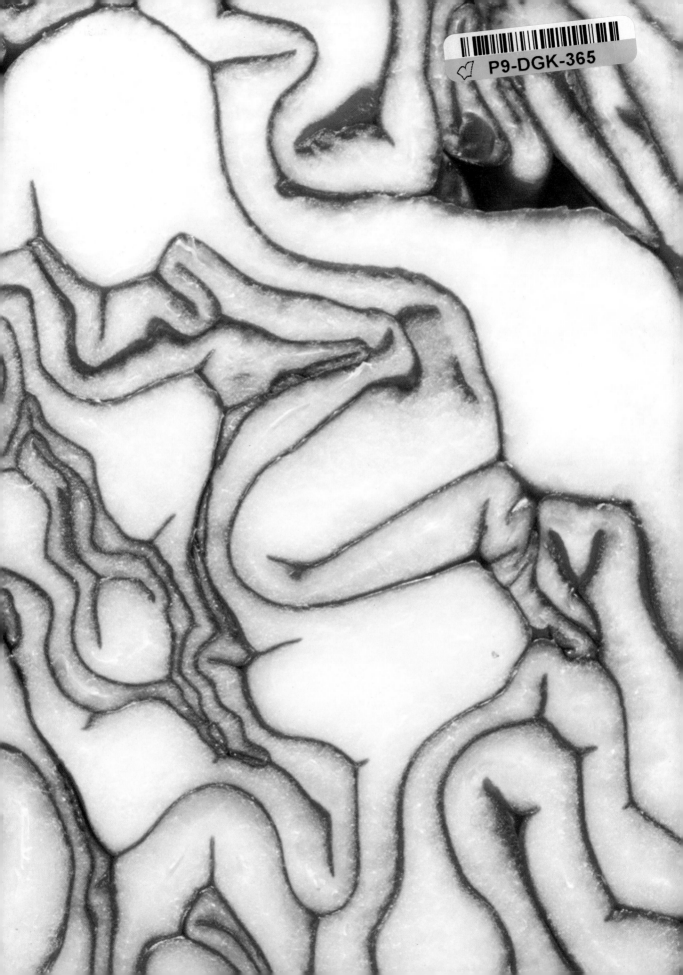

# POWER
# VEGETABLES!

LUCKY PEACH

PRESENTS

PO[...]

VEGET[...]

PETER [...]

AND THE EDITORS[...]

# VER
# ABLES!

## MEEHAN

### OF *LUCKY PEACH*

 **CLARKSON POTTER/PUBLISHERS**
**NEW YORK**

Peter Meehan, editorial director
Mary-Frances Heck, recipe development
Gabriele Stabile, photography
Mark Ibold, food styling & male hand modeling
Hannah Clark, prop styling
Joanna Sciarrino, managing editor
Rica Allannic, Rupa Bhattacharya, Rachel Khong,
    Brette Warshaw, Chris Ying, editors
Devin Washburn, design & layout
DJ Robert "Rob" Engvall Jr., illustrations
Lauren Garfinkle, vegetable portraiture
Kate Slate, copy editor
Special thanks to: Dave Chang, Tony Kim, Sam
    Henderson, JJ Basil, Marysarah Quinn, Miki Tanaka,
    Danny Bowien, Zach Vitale, Lily Starbuck

Published in the United States by Clarkson Potter/
Publishers, an imprint of the Crown Publishing Group, a
division of Penguin Random House, LLC, New York.
crownpublishing.com
clarksonpotter.com

CLARKSON POTTER is a trademark and POTTER
with colophon is a registered trademark of
Penguin Random House, LLC.

Library of Congress Cataloging-in-Publication Data

Names: Meehan, Peter, 1977– author.
Title: Lucky peach presents power vegetables!:
turbocharged recipes for vegetables with guts / Peter
Meehan and the editors of Lucky Peach.
Other titles: Power vegetables! | Lucky Peach.
Description: First edition. | New York: Clarkson Potter/
Publishers, [2016] | Includes index.
Identifiers: LCCN 2016011188 (print) | LCCN 2016022594
(ebook) | ISBN 9780553447989 (hardcover) | ISBN
9780553448443 (eISBN) | ISBN 9780804187749 (ebook)
Subjects: LCSH: Cooking (Vegetables) | Functional
foods. | LCGFT: Cookbooks.
Classification: LCC TX801 .M44 2016 (print) | LCC TX801
(ebook) | DDC 641.6/5—dc23
LC record available at https://lccn.loc.gov/2016011188.

ISBN 978-0-553-44798-9
Ebook ISBN 978-0-8041-8774-9

Printed in China

10 9 8 7 6 5 4 3 2 1

First Edition

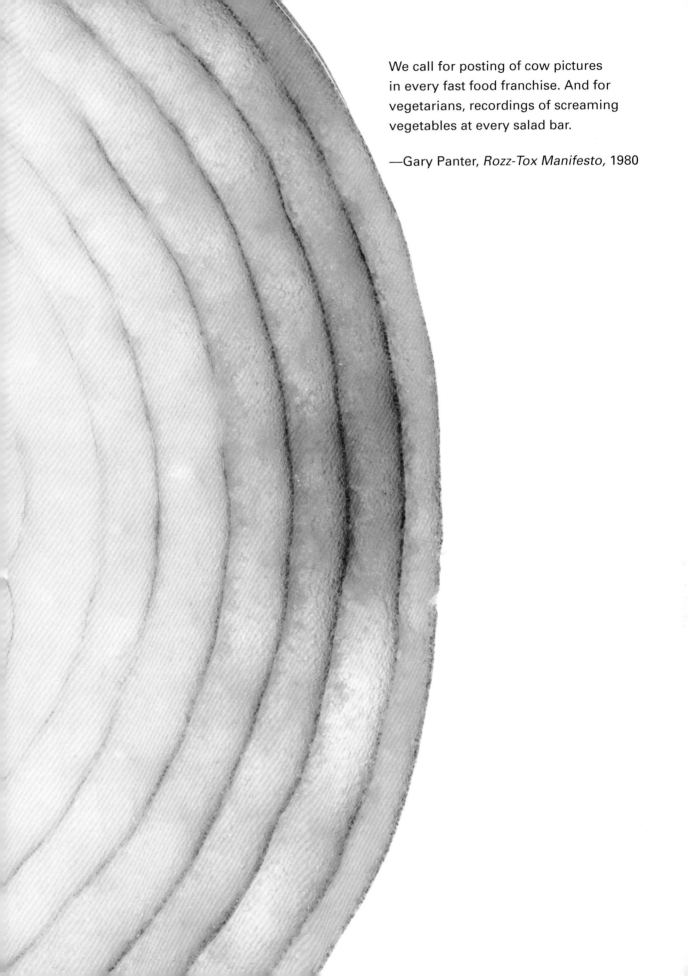

We call for posting of cow pictures in every fast food franchise. And for vegetarians, recordings of screaming vegetables at every salad bar.

—Gary Panter, *Rozz-Tox Manifesto,* 1980

# CONTENTS

# INTRODUCTION

I like a lot of vegetable cookbooks, so when we decided to make one ourselves, it meant I had to think about how to approach vegetable cookery from a *Lucky Peach* perspective.

I didn't want to tell you to cook with what's in season (you have already been told to do this) or to treat your beautiful in-season vegetables simply (ditto). I didn't want to put together a vegetable/vegetarian cookbook for its explicit healthfulness or wholesomeness, though I appreciate and welcome those qualities in any dish, vegetable or not.

I wanted the book to be 98% fun and 2% stupid. I wanted something that took the sweaty, anxious what-are-we-going-to-eat-this-week feeling that sometimes casts a shadow over a Sunday trip to the supermarket and answered it, yelling WE ARE GOING TO EAT VEGETABLES AND THEY ARE GOING TO BE AWESOME.

Look, when I come home from work to a bowl of rice and some steamed broccoli and maybe a little jarred Chinese chili crisp, I'm a happy camper. But sometimes you need more: You need vegetables that are going to be exciting, that will push easy meat- or carb-centric dishes out of the spotlight. Which means they need to be what?

Powerful.

So I knew what we needed. And by that point in the book-making process not only did I want an exclamation point at the end of the title, I was thinking in all caps. Thinking meaningless success-o-slogans like FLAVOR IS POWER and EASE IS POWER and SIZE IS POWER and FIRE IS POWER and POWER IS POWER. **I wanted weeknight all-caps cooking for people looking to eat more vegetable-centered meals.**

What is all-caps cooking? It means center-of-the-meal dishes or certainly **center-of-attention** cooking. **Elote**—a Mexican way of gussying up corn on the cob (see page 156)—is a perfect example of a side dish or an appetizer in the *Power Vegetables!* style. Regardless of what you've got on the menu at your grill-out, you're not going to have leftover *elote*, and if I'm there I'm probably gonna fill up on them and neglect the burgers.

It means vegetable dishes with **real flavor.** Flavorfulness is subjective, and it alone does not translate into power. There were any number of dishes that we tasted in the making of the book that we'd eat and enjoy and then sit there looking at, asking the question: *But are you powerful, little plate of vegetables?* And in that moment, there were many delicious things that were then either cast aside or amped up. For me, *pappa al pomodoro* was too plain, but **pappa al pomodoro crossed with English muffin toaster pizzas** (see page 136) gave my cerebellum the right amount of tingle. Traditional **vichyssoise** barely squeaked by—it's almost too simple—but a variation on vichyssoise made with dashi (see page 138) is clearly a PV.

The idea of what constituted a *power vegetable* mutated over time. The original over-the-top subtitle I had in mind for this book was: "102 turbo-charged recipes that will push the meat off your plate—except for the meat that's in them!"

See, I originally conceived of meaty vegetable dishes standing shoulder-to-shoulder with naturally vegetarian or vegan ones. But as we started to test and sort and select, I thought about what I really wanted to be eating. (I *would* say "what people who buy this book want to be eating," but I can't really judge your situation/needs/wants, since you are, at this moment, a fictional, collective construct propelling this introduction.) And that is why what I thought constituted a *power vegetable* when we set this ship out to sail is different from what I do here on the shore we've landed on. How so?

The biggest and most important change is that **meat is gone**—terrestrial flesh, at least. (There is passing mention of optional bacon in a couple of places; because it is bacon, I felt like that was okay.) But you'll have to pry anchovies and their umami-rich brethren from my cold, dead hands.

There were dishes where this mattered more than I thought it would, like **mapo tofu,** which really gets a lot of power from the little bit of meat that is usually in it, which meant it was just more work than we anticipated to get our mushroom-based version (see page 132) up to par. There were dishes where I thought I'd miss it, like the **French Onion Soup** (page 126), and it turns out it was the vegetables making the dish delicious all along, like that story about Jesus and one set of footprints on a beach, and the onions are Jesus.

I thought that after we published *101 Easy Asian Recipes,* I'd let myself relapse into the old *Lucky Peach* way of running impenetrable-but-interesting cheffy recipes, at least for some portion of the book. We'd examine Jeremy Fox's influential Green Peas in White Chocolate or investigate how to put together a *gargouillou* à la Michel Bras or maybe dig out Roxanne Klein and Charlie Trotter's catalog of high-end raw food cooking. But it came down to the same question: Is that really what we're going to eat at home, what we're going to cook? Is that where the POWER in VEGETABLES is?

I'll go yes and no on that. If you have the means, the time, and the talent, there's a lot to be said for advanced vegetable manipulation: how textures can be twisted, how flavors can be layered, how the composition of a dish can affect how it eats. But at home, how often are you or how often am I going to make that kind of food? I want you to be cooking from this book, preferably all the time. We have borrowed many of the recipes here from chef friends/acquaintances/ crushes, but we've focused on their most doable work, not their most refined.

Instead you will notice there are four spots in the book where we stop with the relentless recipeness of it all and talk to some chefs about what a power vegetable is to them. David Chang, Brooks Headley, Julia Goldberg, Jessica Koslow, and Ivan Orkin all weigh in.

Chef-sourced or otherwise, we've tried to make and keep the recipes easy. **EASE IS POWER,** after all, because what is more powerful than being able to turn ingredients into a desirable dinner with minimal effort? Almost nothing.

And with *101 Easy Asian Recipes,* I learned that readers like knowing the rules of engagement up front. In that book, we did no frying, for example, and banished subrecipes. In these pages, we've allowed ourselves to wade into the hot oil a little more often, and subrecipes have been let in as long as they behave themselves and don't have you jumping all over the book. The specific limitations we put on ourselves for this collection include:

# 1. NO PASTA RECIPES

I love pasta *sooooooooo* much. Too much? Maybe. What I've found over the years is that at home we'll turn vegetables into a pasta sauce as a de facto option. I wanted this to be a slate of recipes that would give me new ideas for dinner and keep me from carbo-loading when I'm not eating meat. That said, nearly everything in here, or some form of its leftovers, would be eatable over pasta.

# 2. NO EGG-ON-IT DISHES; NO GRAIN BOWLS

There is nothing more in vogue at the time that this book is going to press than a bowl of some kind of grain—rice or quinoa or what have you—topped with some vegetables and pickles, crowned with a runny egg. And while we probably could've filled twenty pages of this book with thoughts on them, they're kind of in the same class as pasta: You can put nearly any dish (or leftovers of any dish) from this book on a bowl of grains, nestle some appealing pickles in there and opt in to a runny egg if you like, and you will be stoked and well fed. But I'm not sure you need us to tell you much more about it.

# 3. FISH AND DAIRY ARE OKAY WITH US

After kicking meat out of the book, I was confronted with a choice: Should this be a 100% vegetarian or vegan book? For *Power Vegetables!,* I felt that the answer had to be no. Most of the vegetarians in my life eat fish. (I know that technically makes them "pescatarians," but the number of people who self-identify with that term has to be statistically tiny.) Most eat dairy. And this isn't a book exclusively for those who shun meat—if anything, I'm approaching it as an omnivore who wants things to be delicious first and foremost. But as with climate change, there's no denying that the modern diet leans too heavily on meat and wheat, so it's good to mix things up.

# 4. FRUITS ARE VEGETABLES

What, did you want the book to be *all* potatoes? As any six-year-old can tell you, cucumbers and tomatoes and squash and things with seeds in them are not vegetables. We are saying this to the six-year-old, "Pipe down, honey, we're trying to get dinner on the table."

Okay. That's it. This is and these are POWER VEGETABLES!

**pfm**

POWER

# PANTRY

## BREAD CRUMBS

The power of bread crumbs is not to be underestimated. Think about how much has gone into making them! Flour and water have been married and fermented and baked and the results have probably largely been eaten, except for the hard husk or two that gets air-dried (aka "carelessly left out on the counter") and then ground and stored, waiting to ennoble a dish. All those processes add to the understated flavor and underheralded textural contributions they give to a dish, like the cruciferous medley on page 170 or the stuffed thistle flowers on page 172.

And the *Power Vegetables!* cook should not turn his or her or its nose up at some of the store brands of bread crumbs, like Progresso. I know the image isn't as artisanal as you might want it to be, but the fact that they season those things with milk powder and MSG is only going to make your foods more delicious.

## CHILI CRISP (AND OTHER CHINESE GROCERY-STORE CONDIMENTS)

Lao Gan Ma Spicy Chili Crisp is a jarred "hot sauce" that's a mix of dried chilies, fried to a crisp, along with crunchy little dry soybeans in an oniony, spicy, *ma la,* sugar-spiked oil that is probably the greatest thing sold in a jar anywhere on the planet. (If you're an MSG Truther who refuses to believe the countless double-blind studies published showing that MSG is not any worse for you than salt or sugar, you'll wanna avoid this stuff!) Like its grocery-store sisters Oyster Sauce and Hoisin Sauce, Chili Crisp + a bowl of rice + a plain steamed vegetable becomes an *eating experience.* We only call for it in one recipe (the Mushroom Mapo Tofu on page 132), but I am so comforted by its presence in my refrigerator I would be remiss not to enshrine it in this pantheon of power.

# CAPERS

Who figured out that picking the unripe berries—the flower buds—of thorny little bushes that grow in the rocks around the Mediterranean was a good idea, but only after the aborted berries were salted or pickled into submission? Good on them, and good for us: Capers are a distinctively delicious ingredient that add an animalish umami to anything they're in. (One of the key flavorants in a caper is capric acid, whose name alludes to the aroma of goats—*capre* in Italiano—not to capers themselves.)

I have cultivated a sense of caper perversion for years. I originally sought out nonpareil capers in brine as the older, Francophilic cookbooks that informed my early curiosity told me to. Capers are sorted by size, and nonpareil are the smallest and, reputedly, the best. Changes in fashion, reference literature, and my taste later led me to Italian markets, where I'd buy salt-packed capers that had been picked on the hillsides of Sicily. I started buying larger and larger capers, never noticing any drop-off in or deleterious effects on their flavor.

And over the years, the Fergus Salad (page 89) has been a Christmas Eve standby at my house. My friend Mark Ibold is always in charge of it, and every year we end up so concerned about whether or not we'll be able to find chervil. We don't talk about the caper situation, so sometimes we end up with unfancy, jarred, pickled capers from the crappy grocery store nearest my house. And you know what? The salad never noticeably suffers for it. So my rule with capers is that they're cheap enough and last forever, so if you have the means to seek out some exotically pedigreed specimen, that's okay by me.

But if you can't have the one you love, know that you can love the one you're with and the end results will be just about as good.

# CURRY LEAVES

Curry leaves make only one appearance in this book, in a dead-simple carrot salad on page 90. I had never cooked with them before trying that dish, and they really make it sparkle in an unsubstitutable-for fashion. Then I thought, "Oh man, I gotta learn something about curry leaves so I can sound smart in the cookbook!"

Fortunately, I am an editor of *Lucky Peach*! And there is a writer named Michael Snyder who has filed a number of wonderful stories for the magazine and the website, and one of the latter was a tour of the sorts of things one encounters at an Indian greengrocery. Here's what he had to say:

The name of this small, pointed green leaf comes from the Tamil word *kariveppilai,* which basically means 'sauce leaf' (*kari* for sauce, *pilai* for leaf). Used across southern India and the western coast, curry leaves impart a citrusy and resinous aroma and flavor that's pretty much incomparable to any other herb. Most often, the leaves are used whole and added to hot oil along with mustard and/or cumin seeds and chilies. This either happens at the beginning of a recipe, in a process known as tempering, or at the end, when the flavored oil, known as a *tadka,* is poured over a finished dish (a particularly delicious example of this is in south Indian curd rice, which is both extremely simple and extremely delicious on hot summer mornings).

The word *curry,* used across India to denote any dish prepared with sauce, is derived from the Tamil word that gives this plant its name, and was adopted by the British to refer to the specific mixture of spices that people in the West think of as curry powder. That particular flavor profile has nothing to do with the flavor of curry leaves, or really with anything I've encountered in India at all.

Thanks, Michael! And if you, like me, came across his mention of "curd rice" and thought, *Hmmmm, what is this,* then you are like me. (Are we both Scorpios? ;) ) "Curd" is the name for yogurt in India, and the recipe for it follows. It's simple and a great way to use up curry leaves once you get your hands on them.

# CURD RICE
**MAKES 4 SERVINGS**

|       |                                                               |
|-------|---------------------------------------------------------------|
| **1 C** | basmati rice                                                |
| **3 C** | water                                                       |
| **2 C** | full-fat plain yogurt (not too thick—Greek yogurt isn't ideal) |
| **2 T** | canola or sunflower oil                                     |
| **½ t** | black mustard seeds                                         |
| **+**   | hing (optional; a tiny amount)                              |
| **½ t** | cumin seeds                                                 |
| **1**   | green chili, halved lengthwise                             |
| **1**   | curry leaf sprig (available at Indian grocers)             |
| **¼ C** | grated carrot                                              |
| **+**   | kosher salt                                                |

**1** Combine the rice and water in a large saucepan over medium heat and bring to a boil. Lower the heat and simmer, uncovered and stirring occasionally, until it's overcooked and slightly mushy, 12 to 14 minutes. Let cool, then mix with the yogurt and set aside.

**2** Heat the oil in a sauté pan over low heat. Add the mustard seeds and cook until they begin to sputter, then add a tiny dot of hing (if using), the cumin, chili, and curry leaves and fry, stirring constantly, until crisp—about 1 minute. Add the carrot, stir once, and remove from the heat. Pour into the yogurt-rice mixture, and stir to combine. Add salt to taste and serve as is, or cover and refrigerate to serve chilled on particularly scorching days.

# (LITTLE) FISH (IN ALL THEIR FORMS)

Here are my complex thoughts on this category of ingredients: LITTLE FISH MAKE THINGS TASTE GOOD.

Salted anchovies minced up with fresh greens, herbs, and/or garlic count as one of the most powerful alliances in all of kitchendom, a Mediterranean Voltron. (Don't believe me? Look at what it does for the lowly, unlovable turnip on page 236.)

And then there is fish sauce, my sweet, sweet, beloved fish sauce. I think adding it to only five recipes in this book shows me to be a model of restraint and self-control, because the truth is that it can be added to a wide spectrum of dishes in tiny little dashes to boost their deliciousness without overannouncing itself. The fish sauce vinaigrette heralded on page 166 is one of the most powerful condiments we know of.

# GARLIC

Garlic is a member of the allium family that likes to grow in . . . psych! I'm not gonna write Garlic 101 here because the chances that you don't know what garlic is and have made it this far into a cookbook with plasma balls on its cover are close to zilch!

My thoughts on garlic are these:

**1.** Garlic adds power. Use it. Avoid buying prepeeled garlic because it is gross. Farmers' market garlic from a conscientious and dedicated producer is worth the premium.

**2.** Two ways to sneak garlic into dishes:

**a.** The Raw Rub: We prescribe this in the toasts for Bruschetta on page 69, but if you're of the mind that a dish could use a little kiss of garlic and you're serving it with toasted (or grilled) bread, rub that bread with a cut clove of garlic—not so hard that garlic is present, but just like the bread sprayed a cloud of garlic perfume and then walked through it.

**b.** Confit it: Peel a head of garlic and put it in a small pot with just enough olive oil to float the cloves. Set over medium heat until bubbles form around the garlic (the oil will be about 185°F). Reduce the heat to low to maintain the temperature and confit the garlic until it is very soft and lightly golden brown, about 20 minutes. Drain the garlic, but reserve the oil. Purée the garlic into sauces; it will not announce itself brashly, but instead offer support from the background. I don't think you'd guess how much garlic is in the dressing for the Buffalo Cucumbers (page 84), and that's because it's been cooked this way. And check out Turnips, Garlic, and Anchovies on page 236, where eighteen cloves of confited garlic add a lot of magic in a behind-the-scenes sort of way.

# HING (AKA ASAFETIDA)

Hing is asafetida, the dried and ground resin of a plant that looks like giant fennel and is in the fennel family, a few branches removed. The flavor it adds to food is very umami, very much unlike anything else used anywhere else—it quite literally adds what tastes like another dimension of flavor to a dish. Things like Kaddu (page 168) that call for it can be made without it, though I think it adds power to anything it is in.

In my experience, you never need to add more than the tiniest bump of it, an unmeasurably small amount like $\frac{1}{16}$ teaspoon, which is why we call for it as a + amount, not a measured one.

The smell of hing as an ingredient on the shelf is the stuff of much protestation—too much, I think—and depending on the brand you buy and (I imagine) its freshness or pungency, the power of its aroma can be significant. Also note that this smell is not the same aroma/flavor that comes through when it's cooked, so don't be too shy to consummate your relationship with hing after you bring it home just because it smells unusual before you start cooking with it. It is a portal to power that is especially important to vegetable cooking.

# KOMBU

Kombu is the Japanese name for kelp, a giant seaweed that is nature's MSG shaker. It is the backbone of dashi, the foundational broth of Japanese cuisine, and one of the easiest-to-make ways to add flavor and savoriness to a dish that incorporates a broth or liquid.

Carrot Dashi (page 140) shows how seaweed and simmering turn a juice into a sauce. If you like, you can make a kombu dashi with no cooking at all: Combine seaweed and water and leave them out overnight. The next day, it's kombu dashi! If you're wondering, *Well, what can I do with that?,* you can, first off, use it anywhere you'd use water in vegetable cookery for an extra nip of umami. Like let's say you were gonna simmer up some squash or pumpkin—why not try it in kombu dashi?

And if you're wondering what you could do with the kombu that you use ever so briefly in dashi making—if that's the beginning and end of its run—my answer is no: You can make *shio kombu*! Shio kombu is kelp cooked down in Japanese seasonings, then chopped into a dark green little relish that is excellent snuck into the center of an onigiri and great with simply cooked vegetables or fish. (Or, as my friend Wylie Dufresne uses it, snuck into hamburgers to give them an impossible-to-place umami note.)

# JAPANESE-ISH SIMMERED SQUASH

**MAKES 2 SERVINGS**

| | |
|---|---|
| **1½ C** | water |
| **2** | 3" squares kombu |
| **1 T** | soy sauce |
| **1½ T** | mirin |
| **1** | small kabocha squash, unpeeled, seeded, and cut into 2"chunks (about 1 lb) |
| **+** | kosher salt, for serving |
| **+** | cooked rice, for serving |

**1** Steep the water and kombu overnight the night before cooking.

**2** Remove the kombu. Combine the kombu dashi, soy sauce, and mirin in a small pot. Bring to a simmer, add the kabocha, cover, and cook until the squash is tender, about 25 minutes. Sprinkle with salt, eat with rice, enjoy the simple things in life.

# SHIO KOMBU

**MAKES 2 CUPS**

| | |
|---|---|
| **2 oz** | shredded kombu/kombu strips |
| **¼ C** | soy sauce |
| **¼ C** | sake |
| **2 T** | rice vinegar |
| **1 T** | mirin |
| **1 T** | sugar |

**1** Place the kombu in a saucepan, cover it with hot tap water, and let it sit for 30 minutes to rehydrate.

**2** Drain the kombu and return it to the pot along with the soy sauce, sake, rice vinegar, mirin, and sugar. Cook over medium heat until the kombu is super tender, about 1 hour. If the liquids boil off, replenish the pot with water. Cool completely, then finely chop.

# DRIED SHIITAKES

Dried shiitakes are a must-have. I'm gonna give you a vague tip about buying them: Don't buy the cheapest mushrooms in the store. The more expensive, the better—at least to a point. (You don't need to make a prestige purchase out of them!) If you're at a market that has a range of dried mushrooms, compare the high and low ends of the spectrum and you'll notice better-handled caps in the good stuff—look for plump, full mushrooms. You can certainly work with either, but the fancier ones are nicer, and usually not at too dear of a premium.

The "broth" you can make by soaking a few dried mushrooms in boiling hot water for like 15 minutes is insanely flavorful. They are foundational to the Mushroom Mapo Tofu (page 132), Rice Porridge with Corn and Miso (page 130), and Sichuan Squash Stew (page 134). In that last one, you have the option of just simmering the mushrooms in the soup liquid—the norm core application of the mushrooms—or of blitzing them into a powder, as Danny Bowien, the chef from whom the recipe was stolen, does. That isn't necessary, certainly, but if you do it, grind up some extra 'shrooms and add a pinch to literally almost any Asian-leaning dish you're cooking at a stage when any sort of liquid will have a chance to drink it up. The end product will not be worse for it.

And howzabout what to do with those steeped-and-strained mushrooms? Or what if you're saying, "Pete, I *love* the flavor of these mushrooms! Is there anything I can do so I can just eat gobs of them all the time, with a grilled T-bone steak or just a plain bowl of rice?"

I'd say, "Wow, usually only people who have known me for a long time call me Pete! Also, yes, I've got the recipe right here. It's an oldie but a goodie from the *Momofuku* cookbook, and one of my all-time favorite pickles. It's great straight out of the jar and, as you asked, with just about anything."

## PICKLED SHIITAKES
**MAKES A QUANTITY I'D STORE IN A QUART CONTAINER**

- **2 C** dried shiitake mushrooms, stemmed
- **½ C** soy sauce
- **½ C** sherry vinegar
- **⅓ C** cup sugar
- **1** piece (3") fresh ginger, peeled and sliced into coins of a thickness that will be delicious pickled

**1** Put the mushrooms in a bowl or a pot, and cover with boiling water. Let stand 15 or so minutes (longer isn't harmful, but it's not necessary either). Reserving 1 cup of the soaking liquid, drain the mushrooms.

**2** Combine the mushrooms, soaking liquid, soy sauce, sherry vinegar, sugar, and ginger in a saucepan. Bring it to a boil, reduce it to a simmer, and cook for 30 minutes. Remove the pan from the heat and let the contents cool down to room temperature.

**3** Decant the contents of the pan into a jar and chill well—these taste best straight from the fridge. When serving them, slice the caps up (so they look like the mushrooms on the opposite page.

# MISO

It is probably not true that you can add miso to any food and improve it, but . . . I can't think of any for which it's not true. Check out the hummus in this book (see page 42). What's that making our hummus POWERFUL? Miso. (Idea stolen from Caroline Fidanza from the restaurant Saltie in Brooklyn.) What's making the vegetarian chili that goes over Ivan Orkin's tofu "fries" taste so good? Miso.

Much like it is on an animal farm, all miso is good but some miso is better than others. I vastly prefer Japanese-made miso to crunchy upstart versions made in countries that don't have the Rising Sun on their flag. Buy the best miso your miso supplier (preferably a Japanese or Korean grocery, if you live in the sort of place where that's a reality) has on their shelves; the extra couple bucks is well spent.

The two main types of miso we're concerned with between these covers are white, or *shiro,* miso and red, or *aka,* miso. For the most part (and for all the recipes in this book), you don't need both and you can use them interchangeably; I've mainly kept shiro in the fridge over the years.

Once you've got a tub of miso in the fridge, don't be shy with it. A smidge added to a vinaigrette is smart; a spoonful stirred into mayonnaise makes mayo, already one of my favorite condiments, that much more powerful. Miso plus butter (the two mixed in equal proportions) plus vegetables is always a good idea: Get the vegetables going in a pan in a minimal amount of oil or butter, and when they begin to take on color or get nearish to the kind of doneness you're hunting for, add the miso-butter combo in as generous an amount as your conscience or nutritionist will allow, then stir and sauté to coat. Delicious.

If you have the kombu called for in this pantry and some miso, you're not far from a dinner or a breakfast: miso dissolved in dashi = miso soup. If you make that dashi with a shiitake or two thrown in there, all the better. Then, like the soldiers in *Stone Soup,* you can gather things from around the fridge: Any stray vegetables can be pressed into service, simmered to improve the whole. Stir in the miso right at the end, just before serving it.

And there's miso butterscotch to be made! This is an adaptation of a condiment I first ate when Christina Tosi of Milk Bar used it as a sauce for a deep-fried apple pie. I find it to be criminally good just on plain vanilla ice cream. It's a good use for the end of a dwindling tub of miso, and keeps for weeks once it's made.

# MISO BUTTERSCOTCH
**MAKES 1½ CUPS**

**½ C**   shiro miso
**¼ C**   mirin
**½ C**   packed brown sugar
**6 T**   unsalted butter, at room temperature
**2 T**   hot water

**1** Heat the oven to 400°F. Line a baking sheet with a silicone baking mat.

**2** Spread the miso out in an even layer, about ¼ inch thick, on the lined baking sheet. Bake it until the miso is well browned and quite a bit burnt around the edges, about 30 minutes. Remove it from the oven and let it cool slightly.

**3** Scrape the miso into a blender. Add the mirin, brown sugar, butter, and water to the miso and blend until smooth. You can add a splash more water if the mixture is too tight. Store in the fridge, and nuke or warm on the stove (if you have the patience) before serving.

## SOY SAUCE

There are ten recipes that call for soy sauce in the book, so it deserves a spot up here. My advice about buying it is to head in the direction of Japan, which produces my favorite soy sauces. Do not use low-sodium soy sauce because oxymorons rarely make for excellent condiments. Do not substitute tamari for soy sauce unless you have celiac disease or are trapped cooking in the distant woodland cottage of some sort of seventies-throwback hippie and tracking down a bottle of even grocery store Kikkoman is too much work.

While most of the by-products of working with Dave Chang for as long as I have are psychological scars, there is one thing he's certainly influenced me on foodwise: I use *usukuchi* soy sauce, which is a lighter-flavored and slightly saltier soy sauce that's got extra stuff in it—a little sweetener, often mirin, and I think just some plain salt. It is by no means the only soy sauce to use or the "best" by any measure, but it's got a flavor that just seems right to me now.

My friend JJ Basil, whom I know from his time at wd~50 but who has had a hand in opening all kinds of New York places including Carbone and Superiority Burger, has a house condiment he makes: half soy sauce, half white vinegar, and as much extremely finely julienned ginger as makes sense. It's a winner and a nice thing to find in the fridge when you're starving and need a sauce to make anything (plain tofu, simple veggies, etc.) taste good.

# VINEGAR

Vinegar is an undersung hero in vegetable cookery: Vegetables themselves are almost always devoid of any appreciable "acid" component and most of the fruits that we (or at least I) think of as vegetables are selected for sweetness and flavor more so than their pucker power.

Lemons and limes are great ways to add a splash of sour, but having a robust little family of vinegars on hand—which never go bad, unlike citrus—means you're ready to power up your vegetables at anytime. Vinegars brighten and sharpen flavors—they add a spark to something long-cooked, and nudge out the sweetness of something like a carrot.

Sherry vinegar has long been my sour of power; it's a wine vinegar that's got a touch of barrel-aged mellowness to it. There's little I won't add it to; *Lucky Peach* editor and celebrity chef Dave Chang is the first person I knew to use it in an Asian context, as in the shiitake pickles (page 22) and the tomato salad (page 96) herein.

White vinegar is sharp and aggressive and uncouth; it's the greaser with a pack of unfiltered Pall Malls rolled up in his T-shirt sleeve of the vinegar family. But its unfashionability—wine vinegar is all anybody calls for in recipes anymore—ignores that sometimes you need acid that hits like an uppercut. You'll see it dotted throughout the book.

In becoming so trendy and ubiquitous, balsamic became a meaningless catchall term for a family of syrup-sweetened, colored, crappy vinegars that are, charitably, charmless. But real balsamic, from the area around Modena, is good stuff. I probably would have never reacquainted myself with its pleasures if I wasn't making the Fergus Salad on page 89 regularly.

And there's more to vinegar than just splashing it on things: try adding it to a reducing sauce or a melting pile of onions (as is done with cider vinegar in ABC Squash Toast, page 30) or using it to season a dish that's still hot (like Caponata, page 32) to add a high-acid sparkle that's still gonna shine when the dish reaches a more approachable temperature.

## THE POWER TRIANGLE

If vegetables were superheroes, they'd get their power from a mysterious triad: fat, salt, and acid. Whenever you are cooking vegetables from this book, from outside of this book, or for your teething infant, remember the triad. Taste what you're cooking and literally quiz yourself: Is there enough fat, is there enough acid, is there enough salt?

It is rare, or should be, that the answer is: YES, THIS IS PERFECT I AM A GENIUS LET'S EAT. You can do better than that. A glug or two of olive oil over steamed vegetables can be transformative. A splash of acid into a pan of cooked greens can make their inherent flavor sing. Textural salt, like Maldon, can make food more fun to eat—it's like adding little flakes of flavor! And salt for seasoning is one of those things that home cooks are always reserved about in ways that restaurant cooks aren't. And while I'm not advocating that you make all your food at home Burger King–salty, if you ask yourself those questions before you bring the food to the table, you have one more chance to make it just a little more delicious—and a little more powerful!

# STARTERS

# ABC SQUASH TOAST

This is a squash shmoo that has all the knobs turned up to eleven: maple syrup and cider vinegar and a finishing sprinkle of hot chili make it compulsively eatable in a way that squash rarely is.

The ABC in the title of this recipe refers to ABC Carpet & Home, an exotically priced New York City emporium of mirrored chandeliers and other things I imagine are used by fancier people than I will ever know to decorate apartments they will never live in. The store's first floor was one of the most accursed restaurant spaces in the city, a revolving door of countless dining concepts, none of which ever put down roots, until Jean-Georges Vongerichten took it over and installed (the now-departed) Dan Kluger as chef of ABC Kitchen.

Now it's so busy you can't even get in at lunch, but I remember a dinner there years ago with vegetarian friends, when there were no fewer than FOUR squash dishes on the dinner menu. We ate them ravenously and happily. Then a few nights later my friend Amanda Kludt came over with a big quart of this shmoo that she had learned how to cook from Mr. Kluger, and we ate almost all of it, with spoons and crackers. If you'd like to serve it as they did at the restaurant, smear your toasts with a couple tablespoons of ricotta, goat cheese, feta, or mascarpone, before topping them with shmoo.

**MAKES 8 SERVINGS
(ABOUT 2 CUPS MUSH)**

**1 lb** peeled kabocha squash, cut into ½"-thick half-moons, seeds composted

**6 T** extra-virgin olive oil

**+** kosher salt

**1** large onion, thinly sliced into half-moons

**¼ C** apple cider vinegar

**¼ C** maple syrup

**¼ t** chili flakes

**+** freshly ground black pepper

**8** slices country bread, toasted

**+** scallions, thinly sliced

**1** Heat the oven to 450°F.

**2** Put the squash in a large bowl, drizzle it with 2 tablespoons of the olive oil (more if needed to get it good and glistening), and season with a generous sprinkle of salt. Toss to coat evenly in the oil, then arrange the squash on a baking sheet or two (it should not be crowded). Roast until tender and deeply browned in spots, 20 to 30 minutes. Transfer the squash to a bowl and keep warm.

**3** Meanwhile, heat the remaining 4 tablespoons olive oil in a medium skillet over medium heat. Add the onion and season with a large pinch of salt. Cook, stirring often and reducing the heat as necessary to keep the onions from taking on color too quickly. After 15 minutes, the onions will have collapsed in the pan and begun to caramelize, which is when you will stir in the vinegar and maple syrup. Continue cooking, scraping the bottom of the pan with a silicone spatula to encourage even caramelization and to evenly distribute the deliciousness forming in the pan. The onion will transform into a thick, tight jam. Turn off the heat and scrape it into the bowl with the squash.

**4** Mash the squash and onion with a fork until you have a smooth mash with a few strings of onion throughout. Add the chili flakes and season to taste with salt and black pepper.

**5** Make your toasts, and when they're ready, top each slice with ¼ cup of the squash mixture, spreading it to the edges. Finish with sliced scallions.

# CAPONATA

Here at *Lucky Peach,* in the eternal battle between ratatouille and caponata, between similar-looking eggplant stews, between southern France and southern Italy, we side with Sicilia. Is it the influence of organized crime? Maybe. Is it because the interplay of sweet-and-sour in caponata is more thrilling, more invigorating, than the sunbathed laissez-faire of ratatouille? Yes. As our Italian photographer, Gabriele, who gave us this recipe, says, "Caponata reminds people of ratatouille, but unlike ratatouille, it's actually good."

Caponata is served at room temperature or coldish out of the fridge, but your best chance to get the sweet-and-sour thing right is while it's hot on the stove. Dial in on the balance of vinegar and sugar there, since it's harder to season it as effectively after the fact. Serve the caponata with rustico bread if you're living *la dolce vita,* or with Triscuits if you know that opening up a box and making up a snack is as powerful a power move as there is.

**MAKES 1 QUART**

| | |
|---|---|
| ¾ **C** | olive oil |
| **3** | medium eggplants (about 3 lb), cut into 1″ cubes |
| **1** | onion, finely chopped |
| **+** | kosher salt |
| **2 C** | Simple Tomato Sauce (page 34) or any tomato sauce you like |
| ½ **C** | pitted green olives, roughly chopped |
| ¼ **C** | roughly chopped capers (if salt-packed, wash them in cool water and dry them gently before using) |
| **1 C** | celery heart pieces, sliced crosswise into Cs, with some leaves, chopped |
| **4** | anchovy fillets, chopped |
| ¼ **C** | red wine vinegar |
| **1 T** | sugar |
| **+** | freshly ground black pepper |

**1** Heat a large, heavy pot over medium heat, then coat with ¼ cup of the olive oil. Add about one-third of the eggplant and brown on all sides, about 6 minutes. (Eggplant likes to drink up oil, then stick and burn; keep it moving with a metal spatula, scraping the bottom of the pot as you toss and tumble it.) Transfer to a dish, add another 2 to 3 tablespoons of oil, and repeat with two more batches of eggplant. Make sure to brown the eggplant well—undercooked eggplant is gross, and overcooked eggplant is more or less impossible in my book.

**2** Warm another ¼ cup olive oil in the pot and add the onion. Fold the onion in the fat and season with a pinch of salt. Cook until the onion is translucent around the edges and is starting to pick up some color, about 5 minutes. Add the tomato sauce, olives, capers, celery, and anchovies. Bring to a simmer, then return the eggplant to the pot and add the vinegar and sugar. Gently stir the mixture and let simmer, uncovered, for about 30 minutes, until the vegetables are tender but not falling apart and the stew has thickened around the eggplant cubes.

**3** Season with salt and pepper. Taste the caponata: The sweetness of the onion and sugar should balance with the sourness of the tomato and vinegar. When warm it will be brightly acidic with soothing sweetness, like biting into an early August tomato or a Vidalia onion. Reseason with a pinch of sugar or splash of vinegar while the caponata is hot, as the flavors meld and mellow as it cools. Serve at room temperature.

# SIMPLE TOMATO SAUCE

**Q:** What do you call a cookbook without a tomato sauce recipe?

**A:** *Lucky Peach Presents 101 Easy Asian Recipes*! But you need one for some of the recipes in this book, so here you go. Feel free to throw in a few sprigs of thyme, or sub fresh tomatoes in season. Make it your own.

**MAKES 6 CUPS**

| | |
|---|---|
| ½ **C** | olive oil |
| **6** | garlic cloves, peeled |
| **2** | cans (28 oz each) whole peeled tomatoes |
| **2 t** | kosher salt |
| **1** | large basil sprig |

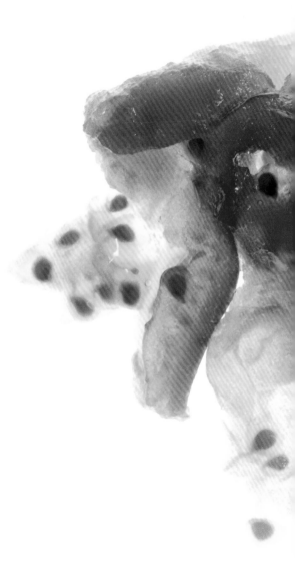

**1** Warm the olive oil and garlic together in a large, heavy pot over medium-low heat. Cook the garlic, turning often, until it turns golden in the oil, about 5 minutes.

**2** Drain the juice from the cans of tomatoes into the pot. Then, one by one, crush the tomatoes by hand and drop them into the pot. Rinse the cans with a splash of water and pour into the pot. Bring the sauce to a simmer, then reduce the heat to maintain a gentle bubble. Cook for 1 hour, stirring and moderating the heat so the sauce neither scorches nor splatters. The sauce will reduce by at least one-third and thicken enough that a wooden spoon will leave a clean line on the bottom of the pot.

**3** Season with the salt and submerge the basil in the sauce. Turn off the heat and cool. Tomato sauce can be stored for up to a week in the fridge or 3 months in the freezer.

# GRILLED SCALLIONS WITH ROMESCO

Romesco, served in this vaguely authentic Catalonian way, is a power alliance of scallions and red peppers. In most situations, scallions have only a supporting role and red peppers jump up and down in the center of the stage; here that dynamic is reversed. The scallions are standing in for calçots, a Spanish member of the allium family—during calçot season in Spain, there are big in-the-field barbecues of charred onions and copious romesco and lots to drink. This is the you-can-make-it-in-your-apartment version of that party.

**MAKES 2 CUPS ROMESCO
(ENOUGH FOR 12 TOASTS)**

| | |
|---|---|
| **1** | head garlic, cloves peeled |
| **¼ C** | olive oil |
| **½ C** | country bread guts, torn into pieces |
| **½ C** | blanched almonds |
| **1 C** | chopped piquillo peppers or roasted red peppers (the jarred Italian kind) |
| **1 T** | tomato paste |
| **1 T** | sherry vinegar or more to taste |
| **1 T** | smoked paprika (pimentón) |
| **+** | kosher salt |
| **2** | bunches scallions (or spring onions or calçots if you live in Spain!), roots trimmed |
| **12** | slices country bread |

**1** Combine the whole garlic and olive oil in a small pot over medium heat. When the cloves begin to sizzle, reduce the heat and confit the garlic at a slow bubble until it is soft and golden, about 15 minutes. Remove the pan from the heat and let the garlic cool in the oil.

**2** Heat the oven to 325°F.

**3** Arrange the bread pieces on a rimmed baking sheet and toast until golden, about 8 minutes. Transfer to a plate to cool.

**4** Brush the crumbs off the baking sheet and arrange the almonds on the sheet. Roast until golden, about 6 minutes. Transfer to a plate to cool.

**5** Fish the garlic cloves out of the oil and transfer them to a food processor or blender. Add the toasted bread, almonds, peppers, tomato paste, vinegar, smoked paprika, and ½ teaspoon salt. Pulse to finely chop and then, with the machine running, drizzle in the garlic oil. Process until you have the texture of loose, chunky peanut butter. Let this stand at room temperature for 1 hour and reseason with salt and a splash of vinegar before serving. (Or cover and chill for up to 3 days. Bring to room temperature before proceeding.)

**6** Heat a charcoal or gas grill to high. Grill the scallions until they are well charred and cooked through. (If you're doing it with actual calçots or bulbous spring onions, you'll want to wrap them in newspaper or towels when they come off the grill—the steam they exude will cook them through.)

**7** Toast the bread slices around the perimeter of the fire, in the cooler areas of the grill, or in a toaster oven. Slather the toasts with the romesco, top them with grilled scallions, and serve.

DIP IT!
DIP IT GOOD!

# DIPS

In the pages and chapters ahead we will deal with many ways of transforming vegetables, of helping them step on the third rail, of harnessing and amplifying their power. But here let us celebrate one of the nicest things about most products from the produce department: You can just eat 'em straight away, right there in the store if you like, raw and unmolested.

But if you take 'em home and cut 'em into polite little bits then you're really on to something! You go from being "girl who was nice enough to have us over" to "accomplished host"; you are serving what my mom always called crudité. And when you add a dip to go *with* the crudités?! That's to basic entertaining what Alec Guinness is to anagrams: a simple way to communicate GENUINE CLASS.

Serve any of these dips with any vegetable you like, and watch the kudos roll in.

## AIOLI

Down there in the South of France they make aioli in a mortar and pestle, which can be difficult—and is one of those cases that Dave Chappelle might label as When Keeping It Real Goes Wrong. Many modern versions rely on a blender, though the mayonnaise will have a hard time spinning once it starts to thicken. Using a whisk is really the best way to achieve the consistency that's going to make you feel like it was worth making.

**MAKES 1 CUP**

| | |
|---|---|
| 3 | garlic cloves |
| ¼ t | kosher salt |
| 2 | egg yolks |
| 1 t | Dijon mustard |
| 1 T | fresh lemon juice |
| 1 t | white wine vinegar |
| 2 T | olive oil |
| ¾ C | grapeseed or canola oil |

**1** Smash the garlic with the side of a knife on a cutting board. Sprinkle with the salt and smash and grind and chop until the garlic is puréed. Scrape into a clean bowl.

**2** Whisk the egg yolks, mustard, lemon juice, and vinegar into the garlic purée. Whisk until the mixture is homogenous, about 20 seconds. Add the olive oil, whisking vigorously, until it is incorporated. Add the grapeseed oil in a thin constant stream. The aioli will thicken and be very creamy. When all the oil is emulsified, use a rubber spatula to transfer the aioli to a ramekin or jar, cover, and chill until ready to serve. The aioli will keep for a day in the fridge.

## BAGNA CAUDA

A hot umami fat bath for your vegetables. Sounds gross until you try it, like French kissing. Particularly good with raw fennel!

**MAKES ¾ CUP**

| | |
|---|---|
| 8 | best-quality anchovy fillets |
| 3 | garlic cloves |
| + | kosher salt |
| ½ C | olive oil |
| 4 T | butter |

**1** Chop the anchovies and garlic together on a cutting board, then sprinkle with salt and smash and rub with the side of a knife until you've turned them into a homogenous paste. Scrape the mixture into a small saucepan.

**2** Add the olive oil and warm over low heat. When the mixture is warm but the garlic and anchovies are just starting to hint at sizzling in the oil, whisk in the butter until melted. Serve warm, over a tea light if you're fancy like that.

## DILL DIP

The vegetable most often served with this dip is the potato in chip form, but it's good with just about everything.

**MAKES 1 CUP**

|  |  |
|---|---|
| 1 C | sour cream |
| 1 t | dried dill |
| ½ t | kosher salt |
| ¼ t | celery seed |
| ¼ t | onion powder |

Stir the ingredients together until smooth. Chill at least 1 hour for flavors to meld.

---

## MUHAMMARA

A Lebanese dip that's nutty and fruity and savory all at once. It's hard to spell correctly but very easy to love. Substitute jarred roasted red peppers for fresh if you're xxxtra lazy: Your secrets, all of them, are safe with us.

**MAKES ABOUT 3 CUPS**

|  |  |
|---|---|
| 2 | red bell peppers |
| 1 C | walnut pieces, toasted |
| ⅔ C | torn bread crumbs (from 1–2 slices bread), toasted |
| 1 T | pomegranate molasses |
| 2 | garlic cloves |
| 1 T | fresh lemon juice |
| 1 t | sweet paprika |
| 1 t | kosher salt |
| ½ t | ground cumin |
| ½ t | chili flakes |
| + | few grinds black pepper |
| ¼ C | extra-virgin olive oil, plus more for serving |

**1** Roast the peppers directly over a gas or charcoal flame or under a hot broiler, turning with tongs so the skin chars and puffs evenly. When the peppers are blackened all around but still meaty and juicy, place them in a deep bowl and cover tightly with plastic wrap. The plastic will puff and then relax as the peppers steam and then cool. Once the concave film shows a clear layer of condensation, remove the peppers. Working over the bowl, rub away the skins with a dry paper towel, then remove the stem and slice the pepper in half. Remove the seeds. Place the clean pepper fillets in a food processor and add any pepper juice that has collected in the bowl.

**2** Add the walnuts to the food processor and pulse until the mixture is smooth. Add the bread crumbs, pomegranate molasses, garlic, lemon juice, paprika, salt, cumin, chili flakes, and black pepper, processing to combine. With the machine running, add the olive oil slowly and blend until the oil is completely incorporated. Scrape down the sides of the processor bowl as you go, adding a splash of water if the mixture becomes very thick.

**3** Serve the *muhammara* drizzled with extra-virgin olive oil in a small bowl, chilled or at room temperature.

# HUMMUS

STOP! Step away from the baby carrots. It's been going on too long, you buying gross hummus in gross plastic tubs from your deli and eating it with gross little whittled carrot nubs. Hummus is a noble and proud thing and when made well, it is the centerpiece of a very social, family-style dinner.

The pursuit of the *PV!* Hummus led down many roads—this final version is a nouveau bastardization, better than what you're getting at the store but perhaps less labor-intensive and craft-obsessed than some well-regarded recipes out there, like one by New Orleans chef Alon Shaya. We've borrowed some aggressive beating from Mr. Shaya (he goes for a full five minutes in the food processor!) and also added a smidge of miso for a secret umami note à la chef Caroline Fidanza. (It is used in her Clean Slate sandwich on page 206.)

Top it with anything that doesn't involve baby carrots: some extra braised chickpeas tossed in olive oil and lemon juice (add another ¼ cup dried chickpeas in step 1 if you want in on that action); some roasted butternut squash or cauliflower; or some crumbled merguez for your meat-eating friends.

**MAKES ABOUT 2 CUPS**

| | |
|---|---|
| **1 C** | dried chickpeas, soaked overnight |
| **1 t** | baking soda |
| **¼ C** | olive oil |
| **1** | smallish garlic clove, peeled |
| **¼ C** | fresh lemon juice (from 1 lemon) |
| **1 t** | kosher salt |
| **¼ t** | ground cumin |
| **½ C** | tahini |
| **1 T** | red miso |

**1** Dry the soaked chickpeas on a kitchen towel and transfer to a deep pot. Toss with the baking soda. Heat the pot over medium-low heat for 2 to 3 minutes, stirring the chickpeas a bit—this is supposed to help soften them or get their skins to come off or maybe help you find true love. Who knows? Do it on faith. When the ritual is complete, add cold water to cover the chickpeas by an inch or so. Bring the pot to a boil and then reduce it to a simmer. Skim off the froth and/or skins as they accumulate on the surface of the water; if it threatens to dry out, add more water as needed. Cook until the chickpeas are soft, 30 minutes to 1 hour depending on the condition and age of the chickpeas.

**2** Combine the chickpeas, olive oil, and garlic in a food processor and blitz them for 2 full minutes. Add the lemon juice, salt, cumin, tahini, and miso and let it churn for another couple minutes. Should be as smooth and light as a puréed baby's bottom. It is best served still warm—and will thicken as it cools—but keeps in the fridge for up to 2 days. Top it well or eat it plain.

# GUASACACA

Look, I have nothing against guacamole. Nobody has anything against guacamole. Everybody loves it. Everybody loves it so much that I know a guy who opened a taco joint and didn't want to serve it and then was more or less forced to by the braying of his customers. Then he noticed that everybody who sat down ordered guacamole and a round of margaritas before they even looked at the menu and this pissed the guy off because these were not the things he worked very hard on UNTIL he realized he was knee-deep in filthy lucre from serving what amounts to very little more than mashed avocado with a little lime squoze on it.

God bless guacamole. But is that all the avocado can do for you? No, of course not. The avocado has got range, range that is no impediment to its creamy, rich appeal.

One showcase for that range is this here recipe, *guasacaca*. It's a Venezuelan thing, a sauce or a spread or a dip, depending on where you're seeing it. It's as friendly a moisturizer to meats as it is to plantain chips, which is how I first encountered it, and how we recommend you introduce it to your friends.

**MAKES 3 CUPS**

| | |
|---|---|
| **3** | garlic cloves |
| **1** | serrano or jalapeño chili |
| **½ C** | chopped red bell pepper |
| **¼ C** | chopped onion |
| **2 T** | white vinegar |
| **½ t +** | kosher salt |
| **2** | avocadoes |
| **½ C** | parsley leaves |
| **½ C** | cilantro leaves |
| **½ C** | olive oil |
| **2 T** | water |
| **½** | lime's worth of juice, maybe more |

Pulse the garlic, chili, bell pepper, onion, vinegar, and ½ teaspoon salt in a food processor to finely chop. Let stand 15 minutes. Add the flesh of the avocadoes and the herbs and process until smooth. With the motor running, drizzle in the olive oil to emulsify, then thin with the water. Stop the machine, taste, and season with salt and lime juice. Cover and let stand at room temperature at least 1 hour or refrigerate overnight. This is best served at room temperature. Reseason with salt and lime juice as needed before serving.

# MAKE PICKLES!

This is an all-purpose idiotproof easy-peasy pickle brine.

**MAKES 2 CUPS
(ENOUGH TO PICKLE 1 POUND VEGETABLES)**

| | |
|---|---|
| **1 C** | vinegar (preferably 4–5% acidity): white wine, red wine, or rice |
| **1 C** | water |
| **2 T** | sugar |
| **2 t** | kosher salt |
| **1 lb** | vegetables |
| **+** | spices |

Combine the vinegar, water, sugar, and salt in a small nonreactive pot. Set over low heat and stir until the sugar and salt dissolve. Remove from the heat and pour the hot brine over vegetables that have been trimmed or prepped and packed into heatproof jars. Let cool slightly, cover, and chill for 24 hours. Pickles will keep up to 2 months in the fridge and peak in deliciousness from 1 to 4 weeks after pickling.

**GREEN BEANS**
(topped and tailed)
+ 4 garlic cloves

**CHILIES**
+ 1 T coriander seeds

**FENNEL**
(thickly sliced) + 1 t chili
flakes + 2 bay leaves

**CARROTS**
(peeled and cut into spears or
coins) + 2 star anise +
1" sliced fresh ginger

**2 MEDIUM CUCUMBERS**
+ ¾ t kosher salt + ½ t dill weed or
1 large sprig fresh dill + 1 t mustard
seeds (Quarter the cucumbers and
add the salt. Let stand 20 minutes
until moisture beads on the surface of
the cukes, then rinse and shake them
dry before packing into jars.)

# PICKLED NAPA CABBAGE

There is a SECRET INGREDIENT in this cabbage pickle and we're not telling what it is!

▬▬ ▬▬ ▬▬▬▬▬▬▬▬▬▬▬▬▬▬▬▬▬▬▬▬▬▬▬▬

**MAKES 8 SERVINGS**

**1** head napa cabbage (about 1½ lb)

**2 T** kosher salt

**3** dried chilies, coarsely chopped

**+** rice vinegar

**1** Cut the head into quarters or sixths depending on its size. Massage the salt in between the leaves, then nestle the cut cabbage pieces snugly into a nonreactive container. Dot the cut chilies in the cabbage pileup. Apply sprinklings of rice vinegar as the spirit moves you, but don't go overboard with it: 2 tablespoons in the whole batch is plenty.

**2** Now, put a plate on top of the cabbage and a weight on the plate. (A plate with a book on top of it? A decorative cast iron doohickey you got at a swap meet? What counts as a weight in your home is between you and God and/or interior designer; just wrap it in plastic if it seems like that would be the most hygienic course of action.) Do not cover or refrigerate this container. Leave it out at room temperature.

**3** The next day, flip the cabbages around and don't drain the liquid they're hanging out in. Return the plate and weight and let it all hang out another half or whole day. At this point the weights can be removed and the pickle can be refrigerated. Rinse, squeeze out, and cut into bite-size (½-inch) pieces to serve.

One of the Powers of Cabbage is hidden from the human eye! That's because the SECRET INGREDIENT is MICROBES! I guess it's not such a big secret, seeing as every-body's into fermenting and pickling these days. I like this pickle because it's so dead simple that it seems like it should be boring as heck when you get to the eating-it phase, but it's not! That's because there's a whole microbial community living on your cabbages and while you usually don't need them to organize and effect change in your salads and stir-fries, they do a great job when you invite them to a town hall with a conducive and supportive environment—which is what this salty, room-temperature strategy of pickle making is. They get to work eating the cabbage and pooping out delicious acids and breaking down big clumsy carbohydrates into smaller, more interesting ones.

# GIARDINIERA

Giardiniera is a term you'll see slapped hinky-dinky on pickle jars near and far, implying that the pickle-smith has gathered up the bounty of his or her garden and preserved said bounty for you, most probably in a vinegary brine. But the only giardiniera that matters is that which is rendered in the style of the Windy City.

See, in Chicago, giardiniera is an OIL PICKLE, which is a very powerful style of pickle, because to the already-winning combination of salt and vinegar it adds FAT. I grew up eating the stuff on Italian beef sandwiches and spooned into Italian cold-cut sandwiches. When I am snacking but not committing to actually making a snack, I will make little beggar's purses of it swaddled in a diaper of mortadella, eaten standing at the kitchen counter. If you hard-roast cauliflower and toss it with generous heaps of this giardiniera, your friends will whisper about what a winner you are behind your back. If you spoon it onto slices of so-so pizza, you will feel better about the pizza and your prospects in life. Giardiniera makes things better and makes life better and gives you an excuse to go online and order a crinkle cutter 'cause you know crinkle cutters are the jam and you've always wanted one. You're worth it and so is this pickle.

**MAKES 2 QUARTS**

| | |
|---|---|
| **3** | celery stalks |
| **3** | medium carrots |
| **2** | red or yellow bell peppers |
| **4** | serrano chilies |
| **½** | small head cauliflower |
| **½ C** | kosher salt |
| **8 C** | cool water |
| **½ C** | pitted green olives, roughly chopped |
| **2 T** | chopped garlic |
| **2 T** | dried oregano |
| **1 T** | chili flakes |
| **1 t** | celery seed |
| **½ t** | black peppercorns, coarsely crushed |
| **2 C** | white vinegar |
| **2 C** | canola oil |

**1** Prep the vegetables: Slice the celery crosswise into ½-inch-thick half-moons. Cut the carrots into ¼-inch-thick rounds with a crinkle cutter. (You can also use a regular knife, but that's no fun.) Stem and seed the bell peppers and serrano chilies and cut them into ½-inch squares. Break apart the head of cauliflower, separating the small stems from the florets. Dice the stems into small pieces, about ¼ inch, then break up the florets into Lilliputian florets that will be delightful to find whole in your pickle dish. Place all the vegetables in a gallon zip-top bag and weigh it. There should be about 2 pounds of "garden" in there.

**2** Put the salt in a large bowl and add the water. Stir until the salt is dissolved. Pour the brine into the bag with the vegetables and seal it. Set inside a roasting or rimmed baking sheet (to catch any leaks) and refrigerate for 24 hours.

**3** The next day, dump the vegetables and brine into a colander and rinse them with cool water. Shake dry and add the olives to the mix.

**4** Combine the garlic, oregano, chili flakes, celery seed, peppercorns, vinegar, and oil in a large saucepan, and bring to a boil over medium-high heat. Add the vegetables and return to a simmer. Remove from the heat and carefully divide the hot vegetables and liquid among the jars. The vegetables should be submerged in liquid. (It is okay if there is a little extra, this is delicious Italian dressing.) Cover the jars and let cool. Refrigerate for at least 2 days before eating. Giardiniera will keep for at least 2 months in the fridge.

# SAUCY FRIED TOFU OR VAGUELY KOREAN WATERCRESS-APPLE SALAD

This traditional Korean sauce is great on fried tofu. When you add some oil and vinegar to it, it turns into a powerful salad dressing.

**MAKES 4 SERVINGS**

## SAUCE

| | |
|---|---|
| **1** | garlic clove, minced |
| **2** | scallions, sliced |
| **2 t** | gochugaru, or 1 t chili flakes |
| **2 t** | maple syrup or sugar |
| **2 T** | soy sauce |
| **2 t** | sesame oil |

## TOFU

| | |
|---|---|
| **1 lb** | firm tofu |
| **¼ C** | neutral oil |

## SALAD

| | |
|---|---|
| **¼ C** | neutral oil |
| **2 T** | rice vinegar |
| **2 t** | gochugaru, or 1 t chili flakes |
| **2 t** | grated fresh ginger |
| **2** | bunches watercress |
| **1** | medium apple (Honeycrisp or Fuji), thinly sliced |

**1** Make the sauce: Whisk together the garlic, scallions, *gochugaru*, maple syrup, soy sauce, and sesame oil in a bowl. Set aside.

### TO MAKE A DELICIOUS TOFU DISH

**2** Cut the block of tofu into about 20 squares: cut it in half and then slice each half into 10 pieces. Transfer the cut tofu to a paper towel while you get to the next step—blotting extra water off will help with the frying, but it's not mission critical.

**3** Heat the neutral oil in a pan over medium heat. Carefully lay as many tofu pieces in the pan as will fit in a single layer and cook until lightly browned, 5 to 7 minutes on each side. Continue until all the tofu is cooked.

**4** Transfer the tofu to a serving plate and top with the sauce.

### TO MAKE A DYNAMIC SALAD

**2** Add the neutral oil, rice vinegar, additional gochugaru, and ginger to the bowl of sauce and whisk to combine.

**3** Toss the watercress and apple in a large serving bowl and drizzle with the dressing until completely coated. Serve at once.

# LOOK WHAT A CUCUMBER CAN DO!

# CUCUMBER-AND-YOGURT SAUCES

With the minorest of tweaks to what you add to the mix, the combination of cool cucumbers and cooling yogurt can take you around the world. *Laban khiyar* and tzatziki are from different corners of the Mediterranean, but they are deployed similarly—as a salad alongside a meal, scooped up with pita, eaten with raw vegetables as a dip. Tzatziki calls for fresh dill and the strained yogurt most often sold as "Greek"; laban khiyar is made with thinner-but-still-rich whole-milk yogurt and dried mint. Raita is a cooling sauce/salad/food that can be an integral component of a meal or a condiment that makes the spread of food you've laid out more lavish. You can add ½ cup of just about any vegetable to this raita and it will be something that has been served in India before; my favorite is raita bumped out with cooked chickpeas (honestly, I used canned) or a chopped beet, since it makes the sauce such a pretty color. Both of those are excellent with fish, should you indulge in the flesh of the sea.

For each the directions are simpler than stupid: Stir the ingredients together. Let the sauce stand for 20 minutes, then taste and adjust seasoning with salt and lemon juice as needed.

## LABAN KHIYAR
**MAKES ABOUT 2 CUPS**

- **1 C**   whole-milk yogurt (not Greek)
- **1**   cucumber, cut into ¾" pieces (about 8 oz), or 3 Persian cucumbers
- **1 t**   grated garlic
- **1 t**   fresh lemon juice
- **1 t**   chopped fresh mint (optional!)
- **¾ t**   crushed dried mint
- **¼ t**   kosher salt

## TZATZIKI
**MAKES ABOUT 2 CUPS**

- **1 C**   whole-milk Greek yogurt
- **½**   English cucumber, coarsely grated (or 1 standard cucumber)
- **1**   garlic clove, finely grated
- **1 T**   chopped fresh dill
- **1 T**   fresh lemon juice
- **1 T**   olive oil
- **½ t**   kosher salt

## RAITA
**MAKES 1½ CUPS**

- **1 C**   whole-milk yogurt (not Greek)
- **½ C**   finely chopped, peeled cucumber (about ½ cucumber)
- **1 T**   minced scallion
- **½ t**   fresh lemon juice
- **⅛ t**   ground cumin
- **¼ t**   kosher salt

**LABAN KHIYAR**

**TZATZIKI**

**RAITA**

# BRAISED COLD CELERY HEARTS VICTOR

Imagine this: It is the languid part of the summer, and your concerns are not about your in-box but that the cicadas are too damn loud or that you didn't apply enough sunscreen. The supermarket near the rental cabin isn't so super, and the local farmstand won't pop up again till Wednesday. So you scoop up some industrial-grade celery at the market when you're buying burger buns and peanut butter and survival staples, and you transform it into this cocktail snack that would be at home in *Mad Men*–era. All the work is done ahead of time so that when your friends show up the next night, you dish it out on plates you bought at a yard sale. You serve it seated, with a bracing gin martini and wash your hands of the responsibility of grilling dinner because, hey, you made the celery hearts Victor. You concede that you first had this as a bar snack at dinner at Prune, in Manhattan, and everyone agrees that place is the best, before you suggest mixing up another pitcher of drinks.

**MAKES 4 SERVINGS**

- **4** celery hearts
- **1 t** black peppercorns
- **3** bay leaves
- **+** kosher salt

## MARINADE
- **4** oil-packed anchovy fillets, minced
- **1** garlic clove, minced
- **1** big pinch of chili flakes, like the ones in pizza shops
- **¼ C** chopped parsley
- **2 T** fresh lemon juice
- **¼ C** extra-virgin olive oil
- **¼ t** freshly ground black pepper

- **+** parsley, for garnish

**1** For this recipe, you don't want the big, fibrous outer stalks of celery, just the second tier of light green, appetizing hearts. Trim the tops without losing the interior bright yellow leaves. Wash thoroughly, rinsing deep into the heads by holding directly under the faucet.

**2** Place the celery in a roasting pan or a wide Dutch oven and cover with water. Scatter with the peppercorns and bay leaves. Season the water lightly with salt, about 2 teaspoons.

**3** Lay a piece of parchment paper over the celery, then cover the pot with a lid or foil. Bring to a simmer on the stovetop—over two burners, if necessary. Reduce the heat to the barest flame possible and braise until the celery is soft and tender when you pierce deep into the base with a blade or skewer, 15 to 20 minutes.

**4** Lift the cooked celery out onto a rack set over a rimmed baking sheet to fully drain and cool.

**5** Meanwhile, make the marinade: Mix all the marinade ingredients together, season with salt, and taste it—the mixture should be bright, assertive, and bracing.

**6** Dress the hearts in marinade and arrange in a single layer in a baking dish. Cover and chill in the marinade for at least a few hours and up to a day before serving. Garnish with parsley before serving.

# LEEKS VINAIGRETTE TERRINE

It is entirely possible and perfectly effective not to terrine-mold your leeks when you vinaigrette them. You boil them as directed in this recipe, then mix up an assertive dressing, and dump it over the alliums. Easy peasy.

But this arrangement of leeks swaps ease for elegance: The composition and eating of the dish evokes steak tartare, the look of the plate harkens back to an era of fancy French food when dishes that looked like this were mainly made with meat. Serve it when you're feeling froofy.

**MAKES 8 SERVINGS**

- + aerosol fat
- **5 lb** small leeks, washed well
- + kosher salt
- **3 T** champagne vinegar
- **2 t** Dijon mustard
- **¼ t** freshly ground black pepper
- **½ C** vegetable oil
- **½ C** capers, rinsed
- **½ C** minced shallots
- **½ C** minced cornichons
- **4** hard-boiled eggs, whites and yolks chopped separately

**1** Coat a 10 × 3-inch rectangular terrine or narrow loaf pan with cooking spray and line with plastic wrap, leaving 2 inches of overhang around the edges of the terrine. Cut a piece of cardboard to fit inside the top of the terrine dish and wrap it in a couple layers of plastic wrap. This will help weight the terrine as it sets.

**2** Trim the leeks' stringy roots away, but leave the root end intact. Using the terrine as a guide, trim the leeks about 1 inch longer than the lengthwise dimension of the dish (discard the dark green tops).

**3** Bring a large pot of water to a boil and salt it. Add the leeks and cook until soft, about 15 minutes. To test for doneness, insert a paring knife into one of the leeks—it should be able to go through the leek with barely any resistance. Transfer the leeks to a strainer and let cool to room temperature.

**4** Stack the leeks lengthwise in the plastic-lined terrine, trimming them as needed to evenly fill it. Once all the leeks are in the dish (it may be a bit overfilled), fold the plastic wrap over the leeks and top with your cardboard cutout. Weight with 2 or 3 cans or a foil-wrapped brick and set the whole thing on a small rimmed baking sheet to catch any overflow. Refrigerate for at least 3 hours or overnight for the leeks to fuse to one another.

**5** Meanwhile, whisk together the vinegar, mustard, ½ teaspoon of salt, and the pepper in a medium bowl. Once combined, start adding the oil in a slow, steady stream, whisking constantly to create a smooth vinaigrette. Taste, adjust as needed, and set the dressing aside.

**6** To serve, remove the weights and cardboard from the terrine. Invert the terrine onto a cutting board, keeping it wrapped in the plastic. Using a long, sharp knife, cut the terrine into 1-inch slices (the ends of the terrine are for you to snack on out of sight of the civilized people you're serving this to). Pool a generous tablespoon of vinaigrette in the center of a plate and top with one slice of the terrine. Remove the plastic ribbon around the leeks and discard. Arrange 1 tablespoon each of the capers, shallots, cornichons, and chopped egg in little mounds around the leeks. Add a grind of pepper and repeat with the remaining leeks and garnishes. Instruct your guests to make a mess out of all your hard work for maximum deliciousness.

# TEMPURA GREEN BEANS

My first jobs in food media were as an event planning intern and a publicist, and the clubhouse of the people I worked for was The Red Cat, Jimmy Bradley's restaurant in Chelsea, where this dish has been a stalwart of the bar menu for more than a decade and a half.

It has all the visceral appeal of something I would have ordered at T.G.I. Friday's (which was my favorite sit-down restaurant as a teen) with the sophistication—or at least a price tag—that made it acceptable in Manhattan. I include it here because it was one of the first restaurant vegetable dishes I thought was awesome, even if now I can see more clearly that it was just playing to my inner fat boy/deer that likes a salt lick. But that's okay, not all vegetables need to be the sort of thing you'd split with your yogini.

■ ■■ ■■■ ■■■■■■■■■■■■■■■■

**MAKES 2 SERVINGS**

| | |
|---|---|
| **2 T** | Dijon mustard |
| **2 T** | honey |
| **2** | egg whites |
| **1¼ C** | all-purpose flour |
| **12 oz** | cold club soda |
| **+** | neutral oil, for frying |
| **½ lb** | green beans, trimmed |
| **+** | kosher salt |

**1** Stir the mustard and honey together in a small bowl. Reserve the honey mustard for serving.

**2** Whip the egg whites with a whisk in a large bowl until creamy, fluffy, soft peaks form. Whisk in the flour and club soda.

**3** Pour 1 inch of oil into a wide, heavy pot. Bring the oil to about 350°F over medium heat. A drop of batter should immediately float to the top and turn golden in about 8 seconds when the oil has reached the proper temperature.

**4** Drop a handful of green beans into the batter, then lift them out one by one, allowing the excess batter to drip back into the bowl. Working in batches, slowly lower one end of the beans into the oil, allowing the ends to partially set and act as floating life preservers for the rest of the bean before letting go. Fry the beans until golden and crunchy, 2 to 3 minutes. Remove with a spider to a plate lined with paper towels and sprinkle with salt. Repeat with the remaining beans.

**5** Serve hot with honey mustard for dipping.

## THE FRESCA
**MAKES 1 COCKTAIL**

And to wash it back, how about a glass of the first thing I ever pitched and placed in the *New York Times*—as a publicist! The firm I worked for had been tasked with popularizing a new product called Hendrick's Gin, and we roped Jimmy at The Red Cat into creating this drink to help us do that. Of course, now Hendrick's is everywhere and in everything and nobody remembers this silly old drink, but it's crisp and refreshing and gives you another excuse to pick up a can or two of Fresca for the cupboard.

| | |
|---|---|
| **2 oz** | Hendrick's gin |
| **1 oz** | aquavit |
| **½** | lime, juiced |
| **½** | lemon, juiced |
| **½ oz** | simple syrup |
| **2 oz** | Fresca, or as needed |

Combine the gin, aquavit, lime juice, lemon juice, and simple syrup in a cocktail shaker filled with ice cubes. Shake, strain into a tall glass filled with ice, and top with Fresca. Why not?

# PICOS
## DEL MUNDO

# PICOS DEL MUNDO

The *Good Cook* series from Time-Life Books—a landmark library of twenty-eight books, published between 1978 and the early 1980s, each with a single focus like Eggs or Sauces or Variety Meats—was edited by Richard Olney, to whom I attribute (rightly or wrongly!) the purple, dry, Europhilic section titles that are part of the series' charm.

And they are why, when I think about this little grouping of versatile dead-simple no-cook tomato salsas/garnishes/salads/snacks, I think about calling it "A Profusion of Tomatoery" or "A Most Accommodating Nightshade." But, alas, I am not Richard Olney and Time and Life have long since been torn asunder, so instead we call these our *picos del mundo*. They demonstrate the versatility of tomatoes. They show that with a handful of ingredients and a sharpish knife there are a world of ways to add plants to a meal, flavor to a dish, joy to life. They are the encouragement you need to expand your salsa horizons.

## PICO DE GALLO

Goes with chips, goes on anything Mexican, vaguely Mexican, or Tex-Mex that you might be eating. Freshly made is worlds better than anything you can buy. Can be accentuated with anything in the kitchen sink: Radishes are good, additional chilies are welcome; one or two pickled carrots fished out of a can of jalapeños make it sing.

**MAKES 3 CUPS**

- **½ C**  diced white onion
- **1 lb**  tomatoes, diced
- **½ C**  chopped cilantro (stems and leaves!)
- **1 T**  minced jalapeño chili
- **2 T**  fresh lime juice
- **+**  kosher salt

Unless it's fresh from the earth like a baby from the stork, put the onion in a fine-mesh strainer and rinse it under cold water. Drain well, then toss in a bowl with the tomatoes, cilantro, jalapeño, and lime juice. Season with ½ teaspoon salt. Taste and adjust the seasoning to fit your needs. Serve with a slotted spoon if you have one.

# KACHUMBER

This kachumber comes to us from the kitchen of my coworker Priya's mom, Ritu Krishna. About it she says, "The basic kachumber recipe only has cucumber, tomato, cilantro, lime juice, and salt, of course. My version has onion as well as a touch of garlic and a green chili to liven up the salad. I find garlic adds a dimension to the salad that makes it very tasty, and most people can't tell it has garlic but they like it." Ritu's daughter Priya says, "You can eat it by itself as a cold/refreshing accompaniment to what is typically a hot/spicy Indian meal (lentils, rice, some kind of sautéed vegetable), or you can mix it in with the hot components of your meal to add texture and acidity."

**1 lb** plum tomatoes, or any other tasty fleshy tomato, seeded and diced

**1** Persian cucumber, diced

**1** small red onion, minced

**1** serrano or jalapeño chili, minced

**⅓ C** cilantro leaves, chopped

**½ t** minced garlic

**1 T** fresh lime juice

**½ t** kosher salt

Toss the tomatoes, cucumber, onion, chili, cilantro, and garlic together in a medium bowl. Just before eating, add the lime juice and salt and mix well.

## *PEBRE*

A Chilean condiment that takes a thousand different forms (some *pebres* are tomatoless), it is traditionally eaten with bread and butter, which is how you should start with it. After that it won't be hard to see that it goes with nearly anything on the table.

**MAKES 3 CUPS**

| | |
|---|---|
| **3** | scallions, finely chopped |
| **1** | bunch cilantro (about 2 C leaves and stems), finely chopped |
| **1** | jalapeño chili, minced |
| **1** | garlic clove, minced |
| **1 T** | red wine vinegar |
| **2 T** | olive oil |
| **½ t** | kosher salt |
| **½ t** | freshly ground black pepper |
| **2** | medium tomatoes (about ½ lb), finely chopped |

Toss together the scallions, cilantro, jalapeño, garlic, vinegar, and olive oil in a bowl. Season with salt and black pepper and fold in the tomatoes. Let stand for at least 1 hour for the flavors to meld. Best after a sleepover in the fridge, once they've all really gotten to know each other.

## *ARAB OR ISRAELI SALAD*

I have no idea how to parse or properly phrase the name of this relish, which is eaten all over the lands at the eastern end of the Mediterranean Sea. It enlivens hummus and provides essential counterpoint to falafel. Like the kachumber, it's also good as a little side salad on its own. If you toss it with a toasted pita cut into triangles and a few healthy pinches of sumac, boom, you've got fattoush salad to eat.

**MAKES 3 CUPS**

| | |
|---|---|
| **1 lb** | tomatoes, diced |
| **1** | medium or 3 small cucumbers, cut into ¼" pieces |
| **¼ C** | finely chopped red onion |
| **¼ C** | roughly chopped flat-leaf parsley |
| **3 T** | fresh lemon juice |
| **3 T** | extra-virgin olive oil |
| **+** | kosher salt and freshly ground black pepper |

Combine the tomatoes, cucumber, onion, parsley, lemon juice, and olive oil in a bowl and toss. Season lightly with salt and pepper and toss again.

# BRUSCHETTA

Bruschetta is the outlier of this bunch. It is not a relish, but stuff-on-bread. Still, since it has the same basic ingredient combination, it felt shitty to leave it out in the cold. Also there is so much weird, bad food passing as bruschetta in America these days, we owed it to our Italian photographer to put this version out there. He notes that "some perverts put parmesan cheese" on their bruschetta, but there was a lascivious twinkle in his eye that makes us think he's secretly okay with that. A drizzle of the sort of balsamic vinegar that costs as much as a college education would not be unwelcome. The main thing, other than not adding in a bunch of extraneous stuff, is to just rub your toasts with garlic, not to put the garlic in the mix. *Va bene?*

**MAKES 3 CUPS (ENOUGH FOR 12 TOASTS)**

| | |
|---|---|
| **1 lb** | tomatoes, cut into ¾" chunks |
| **1 t** | kosher salt |
| **¼ C** | extra-virgin olive oil |
| **¼ C** | packed basil leaves, roughly sliced or torn |
| **+** | balsamic vinegar (optional) |
| **1** | garlic clove, halved |
| **12** | slices of grilled bread |
| **+** | parmesan cheese (optional) |

**1** Put the tomatoes in a large bowl, season with the salt, and let marinate for 5 minutes. Drizzle with the olive oil, add the basil, and toss. Add a few drops of balsamic, if you like.

**2** Rub a clove of garlic on hot, grilled bread and top with some of the tomato mixture. Sprinkle with parmesan, if desired, you pervert.

# SALADS

# TABBOULEH

My first experiences with tabbouleh are hard to talk about. All I know is it came from a plastic tub, from a supermarket or a deli case somewhere, and I don't know if anyone involved in its manufacture could point in Lebanon's general direction on a map. It had a mouthfeel like well-moistened cat kibble tossed with lawn clippings after a rain that smelled like your aunt's dirty dish sponge. It was everything that can go wrong with tabbouleh in one place, and it was served with a spoon, like it was this *delicious* meze that I'd just heap onto my plate and wolf down alongside the toxic grape leaves and chalky hummus that were part of that meal.

Real tabbouleh is a parsley salad that's rounded out with a few other things. Bulgur gives it bass but the parsley should be center stage; it should be flavorful, fresh, deeply green parsley that is finely sliced and not mauled with a dull knife. Do not serve it in an inert pile and expect someone to be able to meaningfully eat it with a fork and spoon or even just a fork. Serve it with lettuce leaves—or if your dining companions are worth it, portioned out into lettuce cups—and see it in the resplendent throne it was destined for.

**MAKES 3 CUPS, ENOUGH FOR 24 LETTUCE CUPS, 4 TO 6 SERVINGS**

| | |
|---|---|
| **1** | large tomato, diced |
| **1 t** | kosher salt |
| **¼ t** | freshly ground black pepper |
| **2 T** | fresh lemon juice |
| **2 T** | extra-virgin olive oil |
| **+** | ground allspice |
| **¼ C** | dried bulgur wheat, preferably fine or medium grind |
| **2** | bunches curly parsley, leaves picked (about 6 C leaves) |
| **1** | bunch fresh mint, leaves picked (about 1 C leaves) |
| **4** | scallions, minced |
| **+** | little gem lettuce, romaine, or another lettuce that feels right to you |

**1** Put the tomato and any juices into a large bowl. Season with the salt and pepper and dress with the lemon juice and olive oil. Add a whisper of ground allspice and marinate for 20 minutes, by which time the tomato should have released at least ½ cup juice. Fold in the bulgur and let stand until the grains are tender, another 20 minutes for fine bulgur and 1 hour for medium grind.

**2** Meanwhile, pile the parsley and mint leaves on a cutting board and give them a few whacks to reduce their volume. Begin chopping away at it, moving from one side of the board to the other and back. Go back and forth 4 or 5 times until the herbs are evenly chopped. There should be about 3 cups of chopped herbs. Add the parsley, mint, and scallions to the bowl with the bulgur and tomato and toss to dress evenly.

**3** Arrange lettuce leaves on a platter and top each with a 2-tablespoon scoop of tabbouleh.

# ORANGED ENDIVE WITH BREAD-CHEESE-NUT MIX

What do the beautiful people eat? They eat this salad when they are at Estela on Houston Street in New York City. What goes through their beautiful heads as they eat it? I do not know. Maybe they think about fashion or about different brands of moisturizers or maybe there is just the sound of the wind whistling in there, a sea breeze calmly blowing.

Regardless, what we have here is salad that is fancier than the average salad because we're serving it as "cups." (At Estela it comes in a bowl, in a carefully arranged helter-skelter fashion that beautiful people can eat without staining their Expensive Clothes.) The flavor is as close to a backboard-shattering slam dunk as pescatarian lettuce cups will ever come, a vaguely Mediterranean alliance put together in a new way by the chef Ignacio Mattos, who has a knack for that kind of thing.

But don't think about the harmony of the orange and the endive or the cacophony of the metaphorical backboard breaking. Think about the wind and the beauty and the perfect little endive boats. Eat, my swans.

**MAKES 4 SERVINGS**

| | |
|---|---|
| 1 C | ½" pieces torn fresh bread, preferably from a country or sourdough loaf |
| + | olive oil |
| + | kosher salt and freshly ground black pepper |
| 2 | endives |
| 4 | anchovy fillets, finely chopped |
| 1 | garlic clove, finely chopped |
| 2 T | red wine vinegar |
| ½ C | toasted walnuts, roughly chopped |
| 2 oz | pecorino cheese, broken into ½" pieces |
| 1 | orange, zested and juiced |
| 1 T | white wine vinegar |

**1** Heat the oven to 350°F.

**2** Put the torn bread in a bowl with a healthy drizzle of olive oil and season with salt and pepper. Toss the bread to dress it evenly, then dump onto a rimmed baking sheet and scatter into an even layer. Bake, tossing every 5 minutes until deep golden brown and crunchy, 10 to 15 minutes.

**3** Meanwhile, prep the endives. With a sharp paring knife, cut a cone-shaped plug from the base of each endive. When you remove the core, the leaves should easily fall away from the head. Remove 3 or 4 layers of leaves, then repeat, cutting and removing another core. This will yield the largest leaves and least amount of waste. (Endive ain't cheap!) If the endive needs crisping, fill a large bowl with ice water and submerge the leaves for 15 minutes. Remove and blot dry with paper towels.

**4** Whisk the anchovies, garlic, red wine vinegar, and ¼ cup olive oil in a medium bowl and season with salt and pepper. Add the cooled croutons, walnuts, and pecorino and toss to coat them in the dressing.

**5** In another bowl, toss the endive with the orange zest and juice and the white wine vinegar. Season lightly with salt and pepper and arrange the leaves on a platter. Spoon some of the orange dressing into each endive cup, then fill each with a spoonful of the bread-cheese-nut mixture. Serve your beautiful lettuce cups. You are beautiful.

# NAM PRIK HED CABBAGE CUPS

*Nam prik hed* isn't a lettuce cup at all—it's a Thai dip that's often served with raw vegetables. But it's not pretty to eat that way, plus I may or may not have been on a heavy-duty leaves-as-serving-vessels kick during the creation of this book. So try it this way, but feel free to deploy it as a raw-vegetable dip down the line. You can use a lot more chili than we call for here, but six chilies was within the comfort zone of most people we sampled it on.

**MAKES 6 TO 8 SERVINGS**

| | |
|---|---|
| 24 | napa cabbage leaves, little ones from down near the heart |
| | Nam Prik Hed (recipe follows) |
| + | fresh mint leaves, torn |
| + | fresh cilantro leaves, torn |
| + | thinly sliced red chili rings |
| + | chopped peanuts |

When ready to serve, arrange the cabbage leaves on a platter and top each with a tablespoon of the *nam prik hed*. Scatter each with a few torn mint and cilantro leaves, sliced chilies, and peanuts.

## NAM PRIK HED
**MAKES 1½ CUPS**
**(ENOUGH FOR 24 CABBAGE CUPS)**

| | |
|---|---|
| 4 | garlic cloves, unpeeled |
| 3 | red Thai or Anaheim chilies |
| 3 | green Thai or serrano chilies |
| 2 | slices (1" thick) red onion |
| 1 | large portobello mushroom, sliced ½" thick, or 6 oz shiitake or button mushrooms |
| 1 | stalk lemongrass, minced (about 2 T) |
| 1 T | vegetable oil |
| 2 T | fish sauce |
| 1 T | soy sauce |
| 1 t | sugar |
| 2 T | chopped cilantro stems |
| 1 T | fresh lime juice |

**1** Heat a broiler or grill to high. If grilling, skewer the garlic and chilies so they do not fall through the grates. If broiling, arrange the garlic, chilies, onion slices, and mushrooms on a rimmed baking sheet. Char the vegetables, turning so they color evenly, over or under the fire, about 8 minutes.

**2** Let the vegetables cool slightly. Slip the garlic out of its skin. Coarsely chop the proceeds from the broiler into a chippy-choppy salad that devolves into chunky paste in places.

**3** Heat the oil in a wok or large skillet over high heat. After a minute, add the chopped vegetables and lemongrass and stir-fry for a few minutes until sizzling hot. Pour in the fish sauce, soy sauce, and sugar and toss to combine. Remove from the heat and stir in the cilantro stems and lime juice. Transfer to a bowl and cool.

# CAESAR SALAD

There are few marriages of sauce and subject more perfect in all of the vegetable kingdom. Romaine is water and chlorophyll in one of their most flavorful and pert collaborations. Caesar salad dressing is roughly as satisfying as bacon. Ours is not quite traditional, though it's not quite a gas-station squeeze-pack level of debasement—it's a Caesar-dijonnaise that will make your lettuce proud.

**MAKES 1 TO 4 SERVINGS**

## DRESSING

| | | |
|---|---|---|
| 2 | | small garlic cloves |
| 2 | | oil-packed anchovy fillets |
| 2 | T | fresh lemon juice |
| 1 | t | Dijon mustard |
| ½ | C | mayonnaise |
| ¼ | C | extra-virgin olive oil |
| ½ | t | freshly ground black pepper |
| ½ | C | finely grated parmesan cheese, plus more for serving |

## SALAD

| | | |
|---|---|---|
| + | | olive oil |
| 2 | C | torn bread |
| + | | kosher salt |
| 1 | | head romaine lettuce, leaves separated and washed |

**1** Make the dressing: Put the garlic cloves and drained anchovies on a cutting board and chop them together into bits. Once they are very finely chopped, use the broad side of a chef's knife to mash and smear the garlic and anchovies into a smooth paste. Scrape the paste from the board and deposit into a medium bowl.

**2** Whisk the lemon juice and mustard into the garlic-anchovy paste. Add the mayo and extra-virgin olive oil and whisk until smooth. Season with the pepper and parmesan once the dressing is creamy.

**3** Make the croutons: Heat a slick of olive oil in a skillet over medium-low heat. When the oil shimmers, shake the pan and at the same time add the bread pieces, a few at a time, until all the bread is in the pan but is not sticking to the bottom. Toast the bread, flipping occasionally so it browns evenly, then season lightly with salt. Pour out onto a plate lined with paper towels and let cool. The croutons should be crisp on the outside and still a little chewy inside.

**4** When ready to assemble the salad, pour half of the dressing into a large bowl. Add the romaine leaves and use your hands to toss them in the dressing, coating each leaf completely. Add another drizzle of dressing and the croutons and toss again. The salad should be generously dressed without feeling dressing-logged.

**5** Arrange the salad on a platter or on individual plates. Sprinkle with additional parmesan and serve.

# WEDGE SALAD

At the height of the kale frenzy of the early twenty-first century, I was in California visiting my very dear grandmother-in-law and she was championing iceberg lettuce as having more vitamins than any other green. I believe the source of this information was a forwarded e-mail and/or something on Facebook, but it speaks to THE POWER OF BELIEF. If you believe iceberg lettuce is a superfood, who's to say it isn't? What is "science" anyway? Combined with a high-protein dressing made from blue cheese and a scattering of low-sugar bacon crumbles, who am I to say this isn't the healthiest dish in this book?

While there are assertions in the above paragraph you may want to pick at, here's one you can't: Blue cheese dressing makes even the palest, least flavorful food powerful. Look at what it does for iceberg! Think about what it could do for your Matchbox cars or a pile of tacks or, if you lose a particularly bad bet, for a shoe!

**MAKES 4 SERVINGS**

| | |
|---|---|
| ½ C | buttermilk |
| ¼ C | sour cream |
| 2 T | mayonnaise |
| 2 T | chopped chives |
| 1 T | fresh lemon juice |
| ½ t | freshly ground black pepper |
| 1 C | crumbled blue cheese |
| + | kosher salt |
| 1 | head iceberg lettuce |
| ½ C | diced tomato |
| ½ lb | bacon, cooked and chopped (obviously optional and not at all vegetarian) |

**1** Make the blue cheese dressing: Whisk the buttermilk, sour cream, mayonnaise, chives, lemon juice, and pepper in a medium bowl until smooth. Add the blue cheese and fold to combine. Let stand 10 minutes, then season to taste with salt. Cover and chill until ready to serve, or keep in the fridge for up to a week.

**2** Core the head of lettuce, then cut it longitudinally through where the core once was, yielding 4 large wedges. (Cut them in half if they're perversely oversized.) Put each wedge on a plate and drizzle with ¼ cup dressing. Top with 2 tablespoons tomatoes and 2 tablespoons cooked bacon. Serve with extra dressing on the side.

# BUFFALO CUCUMBERS

Who would've thought cucumbers in chicken-wing drag could be so good?

This recipe is from Parm, the casual Italian-American restaurant owned and operated by Mario Carbone and Rich Torrisi in New York. Note the use of a perverse amount of long-cooked garlic in a place where you don't immediately recognize/taste/perceive garlic—you're seeing a textbook way these guys goose flavor out of dishes. Use a not-too-fancy blue cheese for this—nothing more outré than Maytag, please. For it to taste right, track down a bottle of Frank's—other hot sauces may work, but it's not how they'd do it in Buffalo, New York.

■■ ■■ ■■■

**MAKES 4 SERVINGS**

| | |
|---|---|
| **2** | long English (hothouse) cucumbers |
| **½ C** | Frank's Hot Sauce Vinaigrette (recipe follows) |
| **¼ C** | peanuts, chopped |
| **½ C** | crumbled blue cheese |

**1** Peel the cucumbers in stripes, halve them lengthwise, seed, and slice at an angle.

**2** Toss the cucumbers with the vinaigrette. They should be loosely, casually dressed. Toss in half the peanuts and cheese, dump the salad out into a serving bowl, sprinkle the rest of the peanuts and cheese on top, and serve.

## FRANK'S HOT SAUCE VINAIGRETTE
**MAKES ABOUT ½ CUP**

| | |
|---|---|
| **1** | head garlic |
| **+** | olive oil |
| **2 T** | finely chopped shallot |
| **½ C** | Frank's RedHot sauce |

**1** Make a garlic confit: Peel the garlic and put it in a small pot with just enough olive oil to float the cloves. Set over medium heat until bubbles form around the garlic (the oil will be about 185°F). Reduce the heat to low to maintain the temperature and confit the garlic until it is very soft and lightly golden brown, about 20 minutes. Drain the garlic, reserving the oil.

**2** Mash the confit garlic with the back of a fork and then whisk it with the shallot, Frank's, and 1 tablespoon of the reserved garlic oil.

BOX

# GRATER = POWER

I don't know where my fundamental and unshakable love of the box grater comes from—maybe it was the unfortunate run-in I had with a table sander in seventh grade woodshop class (the teacher laughed at me and my bloody stump of a finger; I've never trusted a power tool since) or Marcella Hazan rather off-handedly making the case, in one of her books, that washing a kitchen appliance often takes as much time as the time it "saves." The box grater is not a kitchen appliance, and it's not hard to clean, and it transforms food. And, as this short assortment of recipes demonstrates, it is a stupid simple way to turn vegetables from horse food into food that people will enjoy and perhaps raise an eyebrow over, wondering what epicurean trickery you have engaged in. "Oh this?" you can say, like a mechanic who's just fixed a car with his Swiss Army knife, "It's just a little salad I made with my box grater. Nothing to it at all."

## TOMATO VINAIGRETTE

Salad dressing ennui is a real thing. You know the feeling, when you're cobbling together another simple salad, a mix of things like those that you've spent hundreds of nights at the table with, and your mind starts to wonder: *Are my salads boring? I've still got it, don't I? Is it me or the salad? What would it take for me and salad to spice things up a little bit?* Fear not: We feel you. As your salad therapist, I recommend introducing this jazzy tomato concoction to your workday salad bowl mix of supermarket lettuce and ho-hum vegetables. It's not the trip to Asia or the Bay Area you and salad might need (see the Asian Tomato Salad on page 96 for the former; Bar Tartine's Chopped Cauliflower Salad on page 100 for the latter), but it'll rekindle that weeknight spark with little-to-no effort.

**MAKES ABOUT 1 CUP**

| | |
|---|---|
| **1 lb** | red, ripe tomatoes |
| **1 T** | sherry vinegar |
| **1** | garlic clove, smashed |
| **½ t** | kosher salt |
| **2 T** | extra-virgin olive oil |

Halve the tomatoes equatorially. Set a box grater over a bowl and coarsely grate the cut sides of the tomatoes, catching the pulp in the bowl below. Stir in the sherry vinegar, garlic clove, and salt. Let stand 5 minutes. Remove the garlic clove and stir in the olive oil.

# FERGUS SALAD

A box grater and raw beets might make for red cuticles, but it also makes one of my favorite salads of all time. This is the work of Fergus Henderson, patron saint of nose-to-tail animal eating, who is also a vegetable whisperer of the highest order. There is never a time I don't want to eat this, winter, spring, summer, or fall. When I find good-looking chervil around, this is always for dinner, and when I can't, I substitute curly parsley!

**MAKES 6 SERVINGS**

- **1 T**   extra-virgin olive oil
- **1 T**   balsamic vinegar
- **1 T**   capers, rinsed
- **+**   sea salt and freshly ground black pepper
- **2**   beets, peeled and finely grated (1½ C)
- **¼**   head red cabbage, cored and very finely sliced (3–4 C)
- **1**   small red onion, halved through the root and finely sliced (¾ C)
- **1 C**   crème fraîche
- **1 C**   chervil, picked, or curly parsley (because it is hard to find chervil sometimes!)

**1** Combine the olive oil, vinegar, and capers in a bowl and season with salt and pepper to taste. It should be aggressive but not an assault. Toss all your red vegetables in the dressing.

**2** Make the plates: a blop of crème fraîche, a pile of red vegetables, a pile of the herb you've ended up with in a quantity that seems generous and looks good. Encourage your friends to make a mess of this good-looking plate at the table to get the most out of it.

# RITU'S GRATED CARROT SALAD

**MAKES 4 SERVINGS**

|   |   |
|---|---|
| **4** | crisp long carrots (about 10 oz) |
| **2 T** | olive oil |
| **1 t** | black mustard seeds |
| **1** | sprig of curry leaves |
| **1** | large lime |
| **+** | kosher salt |

**1** Peel and coarsely grate the carrots into a bowl.

**2** Warm the olive oil in a small pan over medium-low heat. Add the black mustard seeds; they will splatter playfully so keep the children away from the stove. Add the curry leaves, swirl them into the oil, and remove from the heat.

**3** Pour the oil with mustard seeds and curry leaves into the grated carrots. Squeeze the lime juice into the carrots. Add salt to taste. Mix well with a fork. This is perfectly good out of the fridge, though you'll eat it fast enough that that will rarely be an opportunity you can take advantage of.

# RITU'S GRATED DAIKON RADISH SALAD

**MAKES 4 SERVINGS**

| | |
|---|---|
| **1** | 10″ daikon radish (about 12 oz) |
| **½** | serrano chili |
| **1** | small lime |
| **+** | kosher salt |
| **1 T** | chopped cilantro |

Trim and peel the daikon and coarsely grate it into a bowl. Cut off the stem end of the serrano and scrape out and discard the seeds. Finely grate the serrano into the bowl with the daikon, then squeeze lime juice over the vegetables. Season lightly with salt and toss to dress the vegetables. Fold in the cilantro just before serving.

The grated carrot and radish salads come to us from Ritu Krishna, the mom of my coworker Priya. I was initially skeptical—*this* is enough to make a vegetable powerful?—but the proof was in the crisp and refreshing pudding that was not a pudding at all. If EASE IS POWER (and, to be clear, EASE IS POWER), these are fantastic additions to your repertoire.

# IVAN ORKIN
## IVAN RAMEN, NYC

**PM:** Is it harder to make powerfully delicious vegetables than it is to make powerfully delicious meat?

**IO:** Maybe? I mean good cooking is hard. And a lot of young cooks don't know anything when they show up in your kitchen—they don't know how to cook a vegetable properly and they don't know what the texture's supposed to be.

But I understand not understanding those things: I came up as a cook in the early '90s, I went to the CIA, I worked at a lot of old-school kitchens—and back then no one would say, *Hey, let's make something great for that person who eats vegetables, who doesn't eat meat.* We'd be like, *What a loser, I don't want to have to cook for them.*

There was a lot of testosterone-fueled conversations like that in kitchens. Of course, over time I learned that a vegetable is a beautiful thing to cook and to do it properly takes real skill. Some of the greatest revelations I've had at the world's best restaurants have been when I've seen a chef, like Chris Kostow at Meadowood, transform vegetables in ways I never could have imagined.

I think this notion of vegetable-forward cooking and stuff is still relatively new, in this country at least. Until quite recently, having vegetables on the menu was a response to vegetarians, you know? But I think in the last five to eight years, people are really saying to themselves, I want to eat more vegetables. We have Michael Pollan saying you need to eat 80 percent vegetables and 20 percent meat; we have discourse on eating vegetables.

Meat is more expensive in Japan. You can, of course, go to steakhouses and get a big piece of meat, but it's more common to go to an *izakaya* and order whatever—duck or chicken or beef—and it'll come on a little plate and there'll be six slices of it, and you and your friends will each take a slice or two and chew it while you're drinking your beer. You'll have all these other things, but not the giant hunks of meat that we eat in America.

When I lived with my family in Japan, we would eat two ounces of meat per person. We would get half a pound of steak and I would sear it and do slices of it and put it in the middle of the table. Everybody would have a bowl of rice and they would have some daikon and they would have some salad and they would maybe have a little piece of fish too. That's what we would eat for our dinner.

Of course there's temple cuisine, but that's not what the average Japanese person eats. Right now there's probably a daikon, that giant white radish, in almost every single person's refrigerator in Japan. Daikon's versatility is amazing: It can be shredded, grated, braised, pickled.

In Japan, tofu is in everything. It's in your miso soup in the morning when you have breakfast. It's served in a cube with some *katsuobushi* and soy sauce poured over the top. It's served as *yudofu* in Kyoto, in a hot pot. And it can be completely unadorned in just a very, very light broth that you maybe eat with a little shaved ginger or some soy dipping sauce. Really well-made tofu is delicious. It takes any kind of flavor so well.

# DAIKON WITH XO SAUCE

A note on this dish from the chef Ivan Orkin, who came up with it:

The daikon in this dish is a super-quick pickle that's very easy to put together. I set it off with what I call XO sauce, but the hitch is, it's not really an XO sauce—it's a *taberu rayu*. In Japanese, *taberu* means "to eat," and *rayu* means "hot oil."

I got the original recipe from a website called Cookpad that my wife loves—I've gotten a lot of ideas from it. I'm not that fluent in written Japanese, but I have enough that I can read recipes and do Google searches with my wife. When I read a cookbook, I kind of get ideas, patterns, or outlines.

Within the world of the taberu rayu there are endless variations. Mine starts with onions that have been tossed with flour. They're sweated out with dried scallops, dried shrimp, almonds, chipotle, sugar, and soy sauce. Then I pour oil on top of that, and cook them out for an hour.

I call it XO because it's a name people understand. And it is sort of an XO: It's the idea of cooking these aromatic, extremely rich things in oil. This has that quality, but it's brighter and sweeter. The XO in and of itself is an invented Hong Kong sauce; it's not a classical thing.

**MAKES 4 SERVINGS**

| | |
|---|---|
| **2 C** | rice vinegar |
| **1 T** | kosher salt |
| **½ C** | sugar |
| **½ C** | water |
| **1 lb** | daikon radish, peeled and rinsed |
| **+** | XO Sauce (recipe follows) |

**1** Combine the vinegar, salt, sugar, and water in a medium pot. Cover and bring to a boil over high heat. Make sure the sugar and salt are dissolved, then remove from the heat and let the brine cool completely.

**2** Using a mandoline, slice the daikon into a fine julienne. Put the daikon in a bowl of cool water and soak for 10 minutes. Drain and refill the bowl with cool water. Soak the daikon for another 10 minutes, then drain and rinse. Drain well.

**3** Place the daikon and cooled brine in a big bowl or large zip-top bag. Marinate in the fridge for at least 30 minutes and as long as overnight. Drain well before serving.

**4** Arrange the daikon in piles on 4 plates. Stir the XO sauce well, then top each mound of daikon with a few tablespoons of the XO. The oil from the XO will seep through the daikon and pool around the base of the plate.

## XO SAUCE

This would also be great tossed into a pile of cold noodles!

**MAKES 1 GENEROUS CUP**

| | |
|---|---|
| **1 C** | canola oil |
| **½ t** | sesame oil |
| **¾ C** | yellow onion, finely diced |
| **1 T** | all-purpose flour |
| **2½ t** | chipotle powder (or any smoky chili powder) |
| **1 T** | dried baby shrimp, roughly chopped |
| **1 T** | dried tiny scallops, roughly chopped |
| **2 t** | sesame seeds |
| **3 T** | whole almonds, toasted and finely chopped |
| **1 T** | fried garlic (a purchased product, akin to fried shallots or onions; optional) |
| **1 t** | soy sauce |
| **1 t** | sugar |
| **½ t** | kosher salt |
| **2 T** | chopped garlic |

**1** Combine the canola oil, sesame oil, onion, and flour in a high-sided pot. Cook over medium-low heat, stirring, until the onion turns golden and "puffs," 15 to 20 minutes.

**2** Add the chipotle powder, shrimp, scallops, sesame seeds, almonds, fried garlic (if using), soy sauce, sugar, and salt. Increase the heat to medium and bring to a simmer. Cook gently until the shrimp and scallops turn the deep golden color of the onions, 8 to 10 minutes.

**3** Stir in the garlic and cook for an additional 3 minutes: The sauce will be an oily alliance of little bits, many of which will have taken on the color of the chili powder. Remove from the heat and pour into a nonreactive container. Let cool completely before using. Keeps for weeks.

# ASIAN TOMATO SALAD

This is the dish from the early and inventive years of my life partner Dave Chang's cooking that I'm surprised hasn't matriculated more widely. It is an update of a classic caprese, it is more reliably delicious than said classic salad (sesame oil hides many ills, like the out-of-season tomatoes in this picture), and it is very hard to improve upon this combination if you're trying to invent an Asian tomato salad—something about it feels elemental and predestined. Make it in the summer when the tomatoes are ripe and win at life. Start figuring out where you're getting your shiso (or the seeds to grow it from) now!

**MAKES 2 SERVINGS**

| | |
|---|---|
| **2 T** | extra-virgin olive oil |
| **1 T** | sherry vinegar |
| **2 t** | soy sauce |
| **¼ t** | sesame oil |
| **+** | kosher salt and freshly ground black pepper |
| **1 C** | halved cherry tomatoes |
| **6 oz** | soft tofu, cut into 1" cubes |
| **+** | shiso leaves, cut into as fine a chiffonade as you can manage |

**1** Whisk together the olive oil, sherry vinegar, soy sauce, and sesame oil. Season lightly with salt and generously with black pepper. Toss the tomatoes in the dressing.

**2** Arrange the tofu cubes on serving plates and top with the tomato salad and soy vinaigrette. Scatter the shiso. Forget that Italy exists.

# SNAP PEAS WITH BUTTERMILK AND CHIVES

Buttermilk dressing and raw spring or summer vegetables are just right and simple and good. This recipe comes to us from Daniel Humm, the chef of the NoMad Hotel, and I have removed the flowers from it that he had in there. By all means, scatter your dish with flowers should you have some growing in the garden or if you, like me, are the kind of civilian who buys them at the market for too much money even though your wife gives you the *really?* look every time you do.

**■ ■ ▬▬ ▬▬▬▬▬▬▬▬▬▬**

**MAKES 4 SERVINGS**

## BUTTERMILK VINAIGRETTE

| | |
|---|---|
| **⅓ C** | buttermilk |
| **⅓ C** | crème fraîche |
| **2 T** | olive oil |
| **½ t** | white vinegar |
| **+** | kosher salt |

## SNAP PEAS

| | |
|---|---|
| **1 lb** | whole sugar snap peas |
| **1 C** | shelled sugar snap peas |
| **1 T** | chopped chives |
| **+** | freshly ground black pepper |

**1** Make the vinaigrette: Using an immersion blender, blend the buttermilk, crème fraîche, olive oil, and vinegar together until fully emulsified. Season with salt and use right away or refrigerate in an airtight container for up to 5 days if you're making it ahead.

**2** Prepare the snap peas: Cut half of the whole snap peas in thirds crosswise or in half lengthwise, creating different shapes and sizes. Place all of the snap peas in a bowl and dress with the buttermilk vinaigrette, tossing to coat. (I don't like to do it too thoroughly or I think they end up looking like they are coated in white chocolate.)

**3** Divide the dressed snap peas among 4 bowls. Garnish with chives and black pepper.

# CHOPPED CAULIFLOWER SALAD

Any meal at Bar Tartine, Cortney Burns and Nick Balla's restaurant in San Francisco, will likely trigger a spate of vegetable epiphanies. Fortunately you can turn to their *Bar Tartine* cookbook, a wonderful document that will let you browse through an international and inventive catalog of techniques they deploy in their restaurant.

This recipe, stolen from that book, was one that I tried because it features two things I hate: raw cauliflower and raw button mushrooms. I thought, "This will be the weak link in the book." And you know what? It's so the opposite. It's a beautiful, mature salad, with a bit of movie-magic alchemy that takes an incredibly unlikely cast of characters and puts them together in the picture they were destined to star in. I would make this at the end of the summer, when a filling but chilled salad is often all you want for dinner, maybe with a loaf of great bread near at hand.

**MAKES 6 DINNER SERVINGS
OR 8 SIDE SERVINGS**

## YOGURT DRESSING

| | |
|---|---|
| **1 C** | whole-milk Greek yogurt |
| **¼ C** | unfiltered sunflower or olive oil |
| **2** | garlic cloves, minced |
| **2 T** | fresh lemon juice |
| **1 T** | red wine vinegar |
| **1 T** | honey |
| **1½ t** | sea salt |
| **+** | freshly ground black pepper |

## SALAD

| | |
|---|---|
| **2** | medium Persian or Japanese cucumbers, seeded and cut into ½" dice |
| **1** | small head cauliflower, trimmed into tiny florets |
| **1** | bunch scallions, cut into ¼" rounds |
| **1 C** | cooked chickpeas |
| **8 oz** | button mushrooms, quartered |
| **1** | bunch radishes, thinly sliced |
| **1** | serrano chili, thinly sliced (use less if you're particularly heat-sensitive) |
| **¼ C** | roasted sunflower seeds |
| **¼ C** | each chopped fresh dill, flat-leaf parsley, and tarragon |
| **+** | sweet paprika, for garnish |

**1** Make the yogurt dressing: Whisk together the yogurt, sunflower oil, garlic, lemon juice, vinegar, honey, salt, and pepper to taste. The dressing can be made a day or two in advance and stored in an airtight container, but even if you're not pregaming that far ahead, put it together before you set about prepping all the vegetables and herbs, which will take a while.

**2** Make the salad: Combine the cucumbers, cauliflower, scallions, chickpeas, mushrooms, radishes, chili, sunflower seeds, and herbs in a large salad bowl. Add the dressing and toss to coat. Let stand, tossing occasionally, until the vegetables give off some of their liquid and the cauliflower takes on a silky texture, about 30 minutes. The salad may be the slightest bit soupy: This is okay.

**3** Transfer the salad to a serving platter or bowl, dust with paprika, and serve. Leftover salad will keep in an airtight container in the refrigerator for up to 2 days.

# CELERY SALAD

This recipe is a version of the always-morphing celery salads that my wife, Hannah, makes. They sail between two fixed points, one being a celery salad with blue cheese–smeared toasts at Prune and the other, a little farther down Houston Street, being a celery salad served at Estela. The relevant data points to keep in mind are: celery + blue cheese = power; celery + salty/sour/sweet = power; pistachios in a salad often (but not always!) make it seem fancy, and fancy sometimes (but not always!) = power.

**MAKES 4 SERVINGS**

| | |
|---|---|
| **1** | small wedge firm blue cheese |
| **¼ C** | golden raisins |
| **2 T** | sherry vinegar |
| **2 T** | water |
| **2 C** | celery pieces, thinly sliced on an angle |
| **¼ C** | celery leaves |
| **¼ C** | flat-leaf parsley |
| **¼ C** | roasted pistachios, coarsely chopped |
| **2 T** | extra-virgin olive oil |
| **2 T** | fresh lemon juice |
| **+** | kosher salt and freshly ground black pepper |

**1** Wrap the blue cheese in plastic wrap and pop it into the freezer for at least 1 hour.

**2** Combine the raisins, sherry vinegar, and water in a small bowl. Cover and let the raisins hydrate for at least 1 hour.

**3** When ready to make the salad, drain the raisins from their soaking liquid and place them in a medium bowl. Add the celery, celery leaves, parsley, pistachios, olive oil, and lemon juice and toss to combine. Season with salt and pepper and toss again. Scatter onto a large platter so the salad has some breathing room.

**4** Retrieve the blue cheese from the freezer and use a vegetable peeler to shave off a couple of dozen blue cheese curls.

# CORPORATE JUICE BAR KALE SALAD

Fifteen years ago, kale was nothing, kale was nobody, kale was something planted in decorative winter window boxes and bought in "ethnic" groceries. Now, jeez, kale. Kale kale kale kale. It's the Jenner-Kardashian clan of the cabbage family; all kinds of kale are hot.

And speaking of heat: We used to eat kale cooked, always! I remember the first time I saw a kale Caesar about a decade ago at Il Buco in Manhattan and my mind was blown mainly because nobody ate raw kale at the time.

Well, I'm old now and the kids today expect a kale salad option. This is, in my mind, the basic template for putting one together. Add half an avocado to each salad to make it nicer, and while you eat it, lament the passing of land lines, AOL e-mail accounts, and that paper-clip thing in Microsoft Office.

■ ■ ■ ■

**MAKES 4 SERVINGS**

| | |
|---|---|
| **1** | lemon |
| **¼ C** | raisins |
| **1** | bunch kale, sturdy/hearty |
| **¾ t** | kosher salt (plus a little more to massage the kale) |
| **1** | carrot, horse-sized, peeled |
| **2 T** | olive oil |
| **2 t** | water |
| **¼ t** | grated garlic |
| **+** | freshly ground black pepper |
| **1** | avocado (optional, but come on, you know it's nice) |
| **¼ C** | sunflower seeds |

**1** Cut the lemon in half and squeeze one of those halves over the raisins, which you have foresightedly put into a cute little bowl appropriate for this sort of plumping activity. Let 'em sit and swell while you prep the rest of the salad.

**2** Stem the kale and slice it crosswise into ½-inch strips. Put them in a mixing bowl, sprinkle them with ½ teaspoon salt, and give the kale a gentle little neonatal massage. As it relaxes, you will grate your horse carrot on a box grater. You will grate the carrot into your salad bowl because as your kale relaxes, it will shed some salty green juice, which you do not want in your salad. Discard the juice and pat the ever-so-lightly wilted kale dry before you toss it in with the carrots.

**3** Stir together the olive oil, water, the juice of the remaining lemon half, the garlic, the remaining ¼ teaspoon salt, and a few turns of black pepper. Anoint the roughage with this dressing. Toss. Taste. Salt? Probably. Portion out onto plates, then add one-quarter of an avocado cut into cubes (if using) and scatter a tablespoon of sunflower seeds over each serving. Namaste.

# PIES &
# THE LIKE

# TORTA DI ERBE

This is a mash-up of the filling of our Italian photographer's mother-in-law's classic Roman *torta di erbe* and the dough of a pizzaish Ligurian flatbread called *focaccia di Recco*. The result is a compulsively eatable and respectably veggie-filled pizzetta that you will likely consume while it's still mouth-scorchingly hot. If you swapped out the Swiss chard filling for a scant layer of stracchino cheese, you'd have the real Ligurian deal, though it would be absent of power vegetables. And if you could pry the recipe for Gabriele's wife's mom's torta dough out of her, you'd be a better man than me.

**MAKES 1 LARGE PIE (4 TO 6 SERVINGS)**

### OLIVE OIL DOUGH

| | |
|---|---|
| ⅓ **C** | water |
| ¼ **C** | olive oil |
| 1 **t** | kosher salt |
| 1½ **C** | bread flour |

### FILLING

| | |
|---|---|
| 4 **lb** | Swiss chard (3 to 4 large bunches), stemmed |
| + | kosher salt |
| 2 **T** | extra-virgin olive oil, plus more as needed |
| + | kosher salt and freshly ground black pepper |
| 1 **C** | finely grated Parmigiano-Reggiano cheese |

**1** Make the dough: Stir together the water, olive oil, and salt in a large bowl to dissolve the salt. Add ½ cup of the flour and stir with a fork until smooth. Add the remaining flour in three additions, mixing until fully incorporated. Once the dough becomes too stiff to stir, clean off the fork and knead the mixture into a ball. Transfer to a clean, dry surface and continue kneading until smooth, 4 to 5 minutes. Wrap in plastic and let rest at room temperature for 1 hour or in the refrigerator for up to 1 day.

**2** Make the filling: Blanch the chard in a large pot of boiling, salted water, working in batches if necessary, until tender and bright green, about 3 minutes. Remove the chard from the water and shock in an ice-water bath. When cool, squeeze the chard with your hands to release its liquid and finely chop. Wrap the chopped chard in a clean kitchen towel and twist from opposite ends to squeeze out as much liquid as possible. (All this squeezing action ensures the torta won't be soggy.) There should be about 1¼ cups of properly dried chard.

**3** Place a pizza stone or an inverted heavy baking sheet on the middle rack of the oven and heat to 500°F.

**4** Assemble: Place the chard in a medium bowl and dress with the olive oil and season with salt and pepper. Add the Parmigiano and toss the greens as if dressing a salad, coating each leaf with the seasonings.

**5** Slick a 10- to 12-inch metal pie plate with a little olive oil. Unwrap the dough and cut the ball in half. Stretch one ball of the dough with your hands, as you would for a pizza, until it is translucent and at least an inch larger than the diameter of the pie plate. Lay the dough into the plate, making sure there is a generous overhang. Scatter the greens over the dough, then stretch the second ball as the first and drape it over the top. Tear a few small holes in several places to allow steam to vent. Press the edges together and trim around the edge of the pan to remove the overhang of dough. Drizzle the top of the dough with a few more drops of oil and sprinkle with a pinch of salt.

**6** Bake the torta on the pizza stone until crisp and golden, 10 to 15 minutes. Let cool slightly before cutting into wedges with scissors.

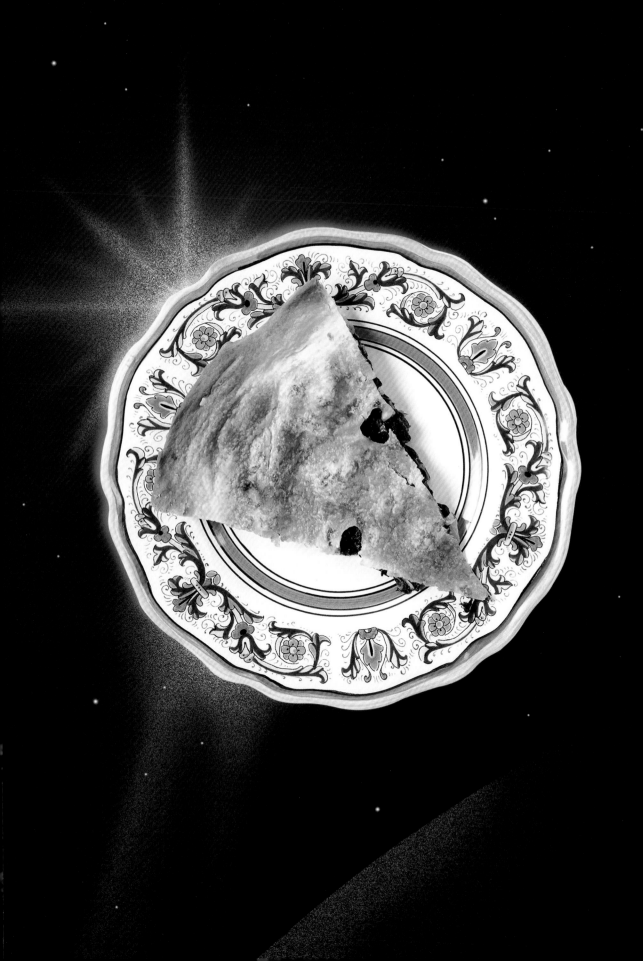

# TOMATO PIE

This is probably the Paula Deeniest recipe I've ever published, though, to invoke a domestic doyenne I am more simpatico with, I think It's a Good Thing. The tomatoes are a front: Though central and titular, they are there to provide lift, lightness, and acidity to a rally of baked mayonnaise and cheese. A couple of real-life Southerners who tasted our rendition of this dish objected to the prominence given to fresh dill in the final mix, but for me the blast of fresh herb flavor makes this like eating a salad out of a buttery crust at a gas station. And I mean that in the best possible way.

**MAKES 8 SERVINGS**

| | |
|---|---|
| **1** | sheet frozen puff pastry, defrosted |
| **1 T** | cornmeal |
| **2 lb** | tomatoes |
| **2 t** | kosher salt |
| **½ C** | mayonnaise |
| **¼ C** | chopped scallions or chives |
| **2 T** | chopped fresh dill |
| **½ t** | freshly ground black pepper |
| **1 C** | grated cheddar cheese |

**1** Heat the oven to 400°F.

**2** Unroll the puff pastry and fit it into a deep 10-inch pie plate (deeper, say, than one of the disposable kind you'd make an ice cream pie in) or a 2-quart gratin dish. Press the dough against the edges (and/or into the corners) and trim the excess, leaving a ½-inch overhang above the lip of the dish. Sprinkle the cornmeal on the puff pastry and pop in the fridge to chill while you prepare the tomatoes. (The cornmeal helps soak up liquid and keeps the pastry from turning to mush.)

**3** Line a large baking sheet with paper towels. Core and slice the tomatoes crosswise into ½-inch rounds. Lay them in a single layer on the paper towels and sprinkle with the salt. Let stand 10 minutes, then blot with paper towels.

**4** Meanwhile, blend the mayonnaise with the scallions, dill, and pepper.

**5** Build your pie: Arrange half of the tomato slices in a shingled layer in the pie dish. Spread the mayonnaise mixture over the tomatoes, filling the nooks and crannies, and top with the remaining tomatoes, arranging in a fashion that pleases the eye. Sprinkle with the cheddar and bake until the pie puffs up in the center, the filling is bubbling, and the cheese is browned, 45 to 50 minutes. Let stand at least 15 minutes before serving—I think it tastes best cooled to room temperature.

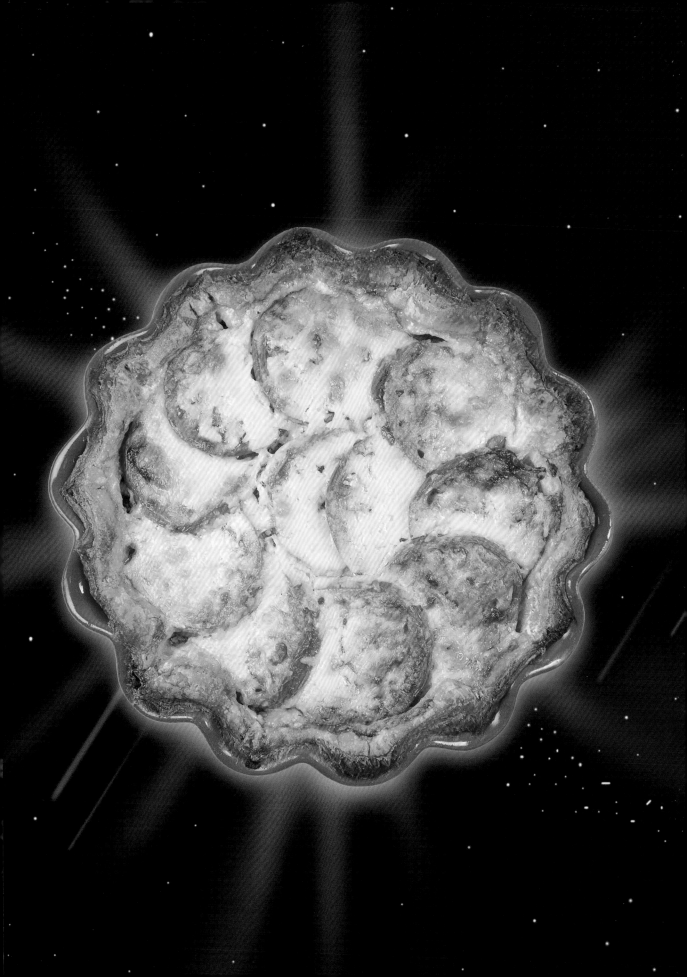

# QUICHE LORRAINE

There was a bestselling satirical book called *Real Men Don't Eat Quiche* that came out when I was a kid. I have no idea what the book was like, but I know its only real cultural legacy was stigmatizing quiche. But look at this recipe—cheese and eggs and a buttery crust, with shiitakes standing in for bacon—and tell me there's any daytime pastry more butch than quiche! Lorraine, the version here, calls on the undeniable power of caramelized onions, but you could easily swap them out for some broccoli and peas and call it a garden quiche!

■ ■ ■ ■

**MAKES 8 SERVINGS**

## SHIITAKE BACON

| | |
|---|---|
| **8 oz** | sliced shiitake mushroom caps |
| **2 T** | soy sauce |
| **+** | neutral oil |

## QUICHE CRUST

| | |
|---|---|
| **1½ C** | all-purpose flour (7 oz), plus more as needed |
| **½ t** | baking powder |
| **½ t** | kosher salt |
| **1** | stick (4 oz) unsalted butter, chilled and cubed |

## FILLING

| | |
|---|---|
| **2 T** | unsalted butter |
| **1½ lb** | yellow or white onions |
| **+** | kosher salt |
| **3** | eggs |
| **1 C** | half-and-half |
| **+** | freshly ground black pepper |
| **+** | nutmeg |
| **1 C** | grated Gruyère or Swiss cheese |

**1** Make the shiitake bacon: Heat the oven to 350°F. Toss the shiitakes with the soy sauce in a bowl until evenly coated. Lightly oil a rimmed baking sheet and scatter the mushrooms in a single layer. Bake the shiitakes for 35 to 40 minutes, tossing occasionally so the mushrooms dehydrate evenly. When the mushrooms have shrunk by about half and are crispy-chewy, remove and let cool. (The shiitake bacon will continue to crisp a bit after it is removed from the oven; if you roast until

completely crispy, the 'shrooms might burn.) Store in an airtight container for up to 1 week.

**2** Make the crust: Pulse the flour, baking powder, salt, and butter in a food processor until the butter is broken down into small pebbles. Drizzle in 3 to 4 tablespoons water, and pulse just until the mixture begins to come together. Dump onto a lightly floured work surface and fold and press until the dough comes together. Shape the dough into a disk, wrap in plastic, and chill for at least 30 minutes and up to 2 days.

**3** Heat the oven to 400°F. Roll out the dough to an 11- or 12-inch circle and fit into a 9- or 10-inch springform pan. Press the dough into the corners, creating a 2-inch-high side. Dock the dough with a fork. Lay a piece of parchment over the dough and fill the pan with baking beans. Bake for 20 minutes, remove the beans and parchment paper, and continue baking until crust is firm and tan colored, another 10 to 15 minutes. Let cool.

**4** Make the filling: Melt the butter in a large skillet over medium heat and add the onions. Fold them over in the fat, season lightly with salt, and cover with a lid. Cook, folding occasionally, until they are wilted from the steam. Remove the lid and continue cooking until they are a light, even caramel color and completely translucent, another 20 to 30 minutes. Using a slotted spoon, transfer the onions to a bowl. Discard any remaining fat in the pan.

**5** Whisk the eggs and half-and-half in a bowl and season generously with salt, pepper, and nutmeg. Set aside.

**6** Build the quiche: Fold the shiitake bacon into the onions, and dump the mixture into the cooled crust. Spread into an even layer, and sprinkle with the Gruyère. Pour the egg-milk mixture over the filling, stopping if the egg threatens to leak over the top of the crust. Bake until the quiche is golden brown and the custard is set, 40 to 50 minutes. Let cool to room temperature before serving.

# TEX-MEX SHEPHERD'S PIE (NO SHEEP)

Almost south of the border, almost a shepherd's pie: This is a faux Tex-Mex artifact that your average extra-terrestrial would guess was the real deal. What's it got to offer? Dinner, in an hour, that's filling enough to make a cowhand happy. You can make it with your favorite cornbread recipe, but the masa harina is the clincher in making the hybrid biscuit-tamale crust!

**MAKES 4 SERVINGS**

## FILLING

| | |
|---|---|
| **2 T** | neutral oil |
| **2** | medium carrots, peeled and diced |
| **2** | jalapeño chilies, stemmed, seeded, and chopped |
| **1** | onion, chopped |
| **+** | kosher salt |
| **2** | cloves garlic, minced |
| **3** | medium zucchini, diced |
| **2 t** | chili powder |
| **1 t** | ground cumin |
| **2 t** | dried oregano |
| **2 t** | smoked paprika (pimentón) |
| **½ t** | ground coriander |
| **+** | pinch of ground cinnamon |
| **1** | can (28 oz) crushed tomatoes |
| **1** | can (15 oz) black beans, drained and rinsed |
| **2 C** | water |

## TAMALE TOPPING

| | |
|---|---|
| **2 C** | masa harina |
| **2 C** | water |
| **½ C** | vegetable shortening or 1 stick (4 oz) unsalted butter |
| **2 t** | baking powder |
| **2 t** | kosher salt |

**1** Make the filling: Heat the oil in a heavy, medium pot over medium heat. Add the carrots, jalapeños, onion, and a pinch of salt and cook until the edges of the vegetables are soft, about 5 minutes. Stir in the garlic and continue cooking until softened, about 5 minutes. Stir in the zucchini and cook until softened, about 5 minutes. Add the chili powder, cumin, oregano, paprika, coriander, and cinnamon and stir. Add the tomatoes, beans, and water and cook, stirring often, until the mixture is thickened, about 20 minutes.

**2** Make the tamale topping: Heat the oven to 350°F. Mix the masa harina with the water in a medium bowl. The mixture will be approximately the texture of Play-Doh.

**3** Combine the shortening, baking powder, and salt in a stand mixer fitted with the paddle attachment and whip until it is light and fluffy. Add the masa dough in three additions, whipping to fully incorporate between additions.

**4** Remove the chili from the heat and pour the chili into a large baking dish or cast iron pan. There should be at least ¾ inch of room at the top.

**5** Spread the tamale topping over the chili, smoothing it evenly to the edges of the pan. Set on a baking sheet and transfer to the hot oven. Bake until the filling is bubbling and the topping is golden brown and set, about 1 hour. Let rest 5 minutes before serving.

# RAJAS EMPANADAS

The world of vegetable pies includes three types: your iconic pie-dish pies (like Tomato Pie, page 110); things in the pizza pie family, which are only called pies because calling pizzas "pies" is a linguistic affectation of the East Coast that is useful for us to appropriate here; and the hand pie—like a Jamaican patty or the handiwork of Fruit Pie the Magician, but with vegetables instead of "apples" and corn syrup. The empanada, most traditionally deep-fried in a crust made with lard, falls into the third category.

Here we use butter in the crust, bake our empanadas, and fill them with a version of Mexican *rajas*—poblano peppers cut and cooked into "rags." Serve them at your next poolside margarita fund-raiser for the neighborhood watch committee or take them on picnics.

**MAKES 12 EMPANADAS**

## EMPANADA DOUGH

- **2 C** all-purpose flour, plus more for dusting
- **1 t** kosher salt
- **1** stick (4 oz) cold unsalted butter, cut into ½" pieces
- **1** egg, beaten
- **⅓ C** water

## RAJAS FILLING

- **3** poblano peppers
- **2 T** neutral oil
- **1** medium onion, halved and sliced
- **1 T** chopped garlic
- **1 t** dried oregano
- **½ t** ground cumin
- **+** kosher salt
- **¼ C** sour cream

## ASSEMBLY

- **1** egg, beaten

**1** Make the empanada dough: Combine the flour, salt, and butter in a food processor and pulse until the butter is the size of peas. Add the egg and water and pulse until the mixture is moist throughout, about 15 pulses. Gather the dough and pat it into a large disk. Wrap the dough in plastic and chill for at least 1 hour and up to 3 days.

**2** Make the *rajas* filling: Roast the poblanos directly over a gas or charcoal flame or under a hot broiler, turning with tongs so the skin chars and puffs evenly. When the peppers are blackened all around but still meaty and juicy, place them in a deep bowl and cover tightly with plastic wrap. The plastic will puff and then relax as the peppers steam and then cool. Once the concave film shows a clear layer of condensation, remove the peppers. Working over the bowl, rub away the skins with a dry paper towel, then remove the stem and slice the pepper in half. Remove the seeds. Cut the poblanos into ¼-inch-wide strips. There should be about 1 cup of strips.

**3** Heat the oil in a large skillet over medium-high heat. Add the onions and cook, stirring, until they've softened and gone completely limp, about 8 minutes. Fold in the poblanos and cook for another 3 minutes or so to let the flavors commingle. Stir in the garlic, oregano, and cumin and season with salt. Continue cooking until the garlic is soft and the rajas are a unified aromatic mass, another 5 minutes. Remove from the heat and stir in the sour cream. Season with another pinch or two of salt; the mixture should be highly seasoned. Let the rajas cool completely before filling the empanadas.

**4** Heat the oven to 400°F. Line a baking sheet with parchment paper.

**5** Dust a work surface with flour and roll out the dough to a roughly 16-inch round about ⅛ inch thick. Punch out twelve 4-inch rounds of dough with a biscuit cutter.

**6** Working with one dough round at a time, brush the surface with a sheen of beaten egg. Arrange 1½ tablespoons of the rajas filling in the center of the round, then fold the dough over to create a half-moon shape. Press the edges together with the tines of a fork. Prick the top once with the fork, then place the shaped empanada on the lined baking sheet. Repeat with the remaining dough and filling. Do not overfill the empanadas or they may split open while baking; save any extra filling for a very delicious quesadilla addition or omelet filling.

**7** When all the empanadas are shaped, brush the outsides with a slick of egg wash and bake until golden brown, about 25 minutes. Remove from the oven and let cool slightly before serving. They are also delicious at room temperature.

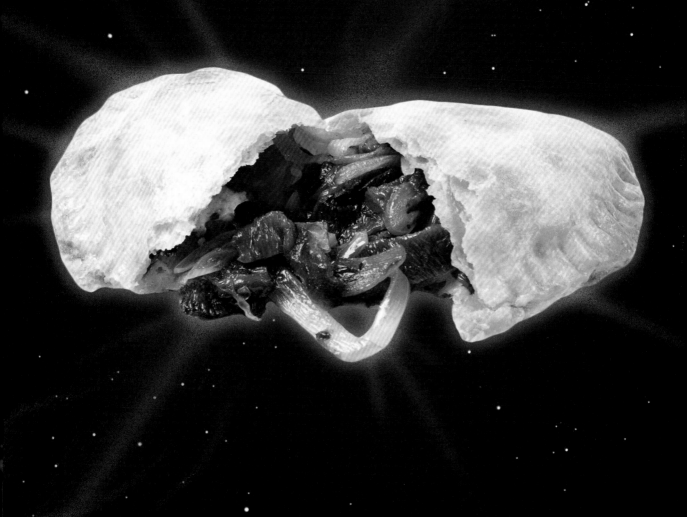

# ZUCCHINI PIZZA

I would like to sell you a bill of goods about how this flatbread conjures the year I spent abroad in Rome, learning about life, love, and myself in the Eternal City, where rectangular vegetable-topped pizzas are as common as headless sculptures of naked men. But the truth is seven degrees less fancy than that. The truth is that once we'd settled into a making-pizza-with-kids routine we needed a version that they'd eat and we'd feel okay about, because even though plain old cheese-and-tomato-sauce pizza is one of the great foods of civilization, sometimes everybody needs a vegetable. This is more of a classic focaccia dough, and if you bake it sans zucchini with just a scattering of rosemary in its place, it will be a lovely accompaniment to Italianate meals.

**MAKES 8 SERVINGS**

## FOCACCIA DOUGH

| | |
|---|---|
| ½ t | active dry yeast, or 2 t fresh yeast |
| 1½ C | warm water |
| 2 C | all-purpose flour, plus more for kneading |
| 2 C | 00 flour |
| 2 t | kosher salt |
| 3 T | olive oil |

## TOPPING

| | |
|---|---|
| ¼ C | olive oil, plus more for the pans |
| 2 | medium zucchini, grated (about 2 C) |
| + | kosher salt |
| ¾ C | grated pecorino cheese |

**1** Make the focaccia dough: Combine the yeast and water in a bowl (or in the bowl of a stand mixer) and set aside to bloom for 5 minutes. With a wooden spoon, stir in the flours, salt, and olive oil until a shaggy dough forms. Knead the dough on a lightly floured surface until the dough comes together, about 2 minutes. Shape the dough into a ball, place it in an oiled bowl, cover it with plastic, and let it rise and ferment slowly in the refrigerator for 24 hours.

**2** Brush one half-sheet pan (or two quarter-sheet pans) with olive oil. Punch down the dough, shape into a ball, and stretch to fill the pan. (If using two smaller pans, divide the dough into two equal pieces and work with one piece of dough at a time.) Cover the dough-filled pan(s) with plastic or kitchen towels and let rise at room temperature or warmer, until puffy, 20 to 30 minutes.

**3** While the dough is rising, prepare the topping: Heat the olive oil in a skillet over medium heat and, after a minute, add the zucchini. Season with salt and cook, stirring occasionally, until the zucchini has released its liquid and the pan looks dry, about 8 minutes. Cool to room temperature.

**4** Heat the oven to 500°F. Dock the risen dough—by which I mean poke it at 1-inch intervals with your fingertips, leaving deep indentations, like you're Beatrix Kiddo attacking Elle Driver. Top the dough with a thin, even layer of the zucchini and sprinkle with the pecorino. Bake until golden and puffy, about 20 minutes. Cut and serve warm or at room temperature.

SOUPS/
SOUPY

# HANNAH'S BORSCHT

As a signifier, borscht lacks any sex appeal: It conjures grandmas in babushkas and guys who guffaw at Jackie Mason jokes. But in real life, borscht is a stunner—or this one is. Why? Because we cook the beets in brine instead of water and use some of that brine in the soup too. It comes to the table in a jaw-dropping shade of fuchsia, a color that's psychedelic and happy-making (and that will also ruin at least one person's shirt during the course of a meal). At my house, borscht is made early in the day during the summer, then put in the fridge to chill. Come eating time, we put the pot out with a ladle stuck into it and lay out a czar-worthy spread of herbs and eggs so that eaters can finish their bowls as they see fit. With butter and rye bread (and maybe a salad if the garden is in swing), there's little better to beat the heat.

**MAKES 8 SERVINGS (ABOUT 4 QUARTS)**

**2 lb** beets, topped and tailed

**1 C** white vinegar

**¼ C** sugar

**1 T** kosher salt

**1** large cucumber (about 12 oz), peeled

**½ C** chopped scallions (about 4), plus more for garnish

**3 T** finely chopped fresh dill, plus more for garnish

**1 T** fresh lemon juice

**3 C** cold buttermilk

**+** freshly ground black pepper

**+** sour cream or crème fraîche, for serving

**+** quartered hard-boiled eggs

**1** Fit the beets, vinegar, sugar, and salt in a snug single layer in a medium pot and add enough water to just cover the beets (3 to 4 cups). Bring to a boil over medium-high heat, then reduce the heat and simmer until the beets are tender, about 45 minutes, depending on their size. Add water as needed to keep the beets covered in brine.

**2** Reserving the brine, remove the beets, and when cool enough to handle, wipe off their skins with a dry paper towel—that's all you need to peel them. (Your hands will eventually return to a normal color; this is the price borscht extracts.)

**3** Grate the beets on the coarse side of a box grater into a large bowl. Grate the cucumber into the bowl with the beets and add the scallions, dill, lemon juice, and 2 cups of the reserved brine. Stir and fold the mixture with a spoon. Slowly add the buttermilk and stir to combine. Add salt and pepper to taste—it should be assertively seasoned. Add up to 1 cup of brine to thin the soup.

**4** Refrigerate the soup until very cold, at least 2 hours and up to 3 days. Serve in bowls with a dollop of sour cream, a sprinkle of scallions and dill, and a few pieces of hard-boiled egg. Freshly ground black pepper is usually a good idea too.

# CARROT-JUICE CURRY

There are a few more components to this dish than others in the book, but type A cooks should have no problem managing the mise en place: Each component is simple to bring together. It's a vaguely Asian "fancy" dish for a night when you've got a vegetarian to impress.

■■ ■■ ■■■■

**MAKES 4 (MAIN-COURSE) SERVINGS**

## CURRY BASE
- **1** can (15 oz) coconut milk, refrigerated for 30 minutes
- **2** garlic cloves, smashed
- **1** piece (1") fresh ginger, peeled and smashed
- **¼ C** Thai red curry paste (jarred or canned)
- **1** stalk lemongrass, smashed and tied into a knot
- **2 C** carrot juice

## ROASTED VEGETABLES
- **2 lb** mixed vegetables (such as zucchini, okra, bell peppers, cauliflower, carrots, baby corn), cut into bite-size pieces
- **2 T** neutral oil
- **+** kosher salt

## SEEDED BROWN BUTTER
- **4 T** unsalted butter
- **1 T** black mustard seeds
- **1 T** sesame seeds
- **½ t** chili flakes
- **4** kaffir lime leaves or ½ t grated lime zest

## ASSEMBLY
- **+** cooked rice noodles (optional), or serve with jasmine rice on the side
- **+** scallions, sliced
- **+** cilantro, picked
- **+** Thai basil, torn
- **+** toasted unsweetened coconut flakes (optional)

**1** Make the curry base: Open the cold can of coconut milk and scoop out the solidified cream from the watery milk below. Set both aside separately.

**2** Melt the coconut cream in a heavy saucepan over medium heat. Add the garlic, ginger, and curry paste, and let bubble for 8 to 10 minutes, stirring every minute or so, until the reddened coconut oil separates from the mass. Stir in the lemongrass and then the coconut milk and carrot juice. Simmer until reduced by one-third, about 15 minutes. Remove from the heat and let stand for 15 minutes. Strain and proceed.

**3** Roast the vegetables: Heat the oven to 425°F.

**4** Combine your vegetables in a bowl and toss them with the oil and a large pinch of salt. Arrange them on a rimmed baking sheet or two—they shouldn't be crowded—and roast until browned and just cooked through, about 25 minutes.

**5** Meanwhile make the seeded brown butter: Melt the butter in a small saucepan over medium heat. Add the mustard and sesame seeds and cook, shaking the pan to brown the milk solids evenly, 1½ to 3 minutes. The mustard seeds may splatter and pop; briefly cover the pan or remove from the heat if they get out of hand. When the butter solids are the color of a hazelnut skin, remove from the heat. Stir in the chili flakes and lime leaves.

**6** Put it together: If using noodles, make a little bed of them in the bottom of a warmed, shallow bowl. Arrange a pile of vegetables in the middle, then pour some of the curry sauce around the base of the dish, making a little swimming pool for the vegetable kiddos. Top with the scallions and herbs and, if desired, a sprinkle of coconut flakes. Stir the butter to distribute the seeds, then drizzle over the dish. Serve hot.

# FRENCH ONION SOUP

When someone proposed French onion soup made without beef stock, I protested, "Mais non! Ce n'est pas possible!" Except when I try to say French words it sounds like I'm gargling with dog kibble, so no one heard or heeded me, and the recipe was attempted against my inscrutable protestations. And *comme par chance, c'est bon, c'est très bon!* Spare the cow and praise the onion!

**MAKES 4 SERVINGS**

| | |
|---|---|
| **3 T** | unsalted butter, plus more for the toasts |
| **1 T** | olive oil |
| **2 lb** | yellow onions, thinly sliced (about 8 C) |
| **1 t** | kosher salt |
| **1 t** | sugar |
| **½ C** | white wine |
| **2 T** | all-purpose flour |
| **6 C** | Brown Vegetable Stock (page 128) or some lesser concoction, warmed |
| **2 T** | Calvados or applejack (optional) |
| **4** | slices sourdough bread |
| **1** | garlic clove, halved |
| **½ C** | grated Gruyère cheese |

**1** Caramelize the onions: Melt the butter with the olive oil in a large, heavy pot over medium-low heat. Add the onions and fold them to coat in fat. Cover the pot and sweat the onions until they collapse, about 15 minutes. Uncover and sprinkle the onions with the salt and sugar. Continue cooking the onions, uncovered, turning them over on themselves every few minutes with a spatula or spoon. Use the spatula to smooth the ever-darkening mass of onions into an even layer and to keep loose strands from sticking and burning to the edge of the pot. As the onions cook, the bottom of the pan should remain clean, without building up any scorched, stuck bits of onion. If matter builds up that can't be scraped away with the spatula, add a few drops of water to the spot and work it away. Cook the onions until they are an even, dark caramel color. This will take 30 to 45 minutes. Don't stray too far from the stove during this process.

**2** Add the white wine to the onions and simmer, scraping up any browned bits in the bottom of the pot, until the wine has evaporated. Sprinkle the flour on top of the mixture, and fold it into the onions. When the flour is fully incorporated—meaning it has more or less disappeared—add the stock and stir gently to combine. Continue stirring, bringing the soup to a simmer; it will thicken slightly as the flour warms. Simmer gently, with the pot partially covered, for 45 minutes. Stir in the Calvados (if using) and continue simmering for 10 minutes. (The soup can be made 1 day ahead to this point, and will taste better if rested overnight.)

**3** Toast the bread, rub it with a garlic clove, and spread it with a little butter. Divide the soup among bowls, and float the toast on top. Sprinkle with the Gruyère and serve.

# BROWN VEGETABLE STOCK

**MAKES 6 CUPS**

| | |
|---|---|
| **2 lb** | yellow onions |
| **1 T** | vegetable oil |
| **1 lb** | carrots, peeled and cut into 2″ pieces |
| **1 lb** | celery, cut into 2″ pieces |
| **½** | bunch parsley stems (about 1 C) |
| **1 T** | peppercorns |
| **3** | bay leaves |

**1** Peel away the loose skins of the onions, leaving 1 to 2 layers of firmly wrapped skin. Trim away any large or dirty roots without piercing the flesh of the onions. Cut the onions in half along the equator and rub the cut side with a few drops of vegetable oil. Heat a stockpot over medium-high heat and lay the onions cut side down into the pot. Cook them until they are very dark brown but not quite burned, about 6 minutes. (Take care not to scorch the onions or the pot, which will make the stock taste bitter. If it happens, pause and wash out the pot.)

**2** When the onions are pleasantly browned, flip them, add the carrots and celery, and 12 cups of cold water. Bring to a simmer, skimming any froth that collects on the surface of the water. Simmer for 20 minutes, then add the parsley stems, peppercorns, and bay leaves. Continue simmering until reduced by half, another 20 minutes, then remove from the heat and let steep for 10 minutes. Strain through a fine-mesh strainer and discard the solids.

# RICE PORRIDGE WITH CORN AND MISO

Forget oatmeal, this is the *Power Vegetables!* way to start the day.

While you should, of course, make this Japan-easy porridge *exactly* as prescribed here, I will concede that any rice will work, any color miso will work, and should you want to make it during the (significant) times of the year when corn isn't worth buying fresh, you can use frozen corn kernels, so long as you bolster that stock in step 1. Any dashi or veg broth will do, or up the shiitake quantity and simmering time, and you'll be just fine.

**■ ■ ■**

**MAKES 4 SERVINGS**

| | |
|---|---|
| **3** | ears corn, shucked |
| **4–5 C** | water |
| **2** | scallions, white and green parts separated, greens sliced |
| **2** | garlic cloves, smashed |
| **1** | piece (1") fresh ginger, peeled and smashed |
| **2** | dried shiitake mushrooms |
| **1½ C** | cooked short-grain rice (leftover is A-okay) |
| **2 T** | red miso |
| **2 T** | unsalted butter |
| **+** | soy sauce or black vinegar |

**1** Make the corn broth: Cut the kernels from the cobs. Set the kernels aside and transfer the cobs to a large saucepan. Add the water, scallion whites, garlic, ginger, and shiitakes. Bring to a boil, then lower the heat and simmer for 20 minutes.

**2** Strain the solids out of the broth and pick the shiitakes out from the strainer. Remove and discard the shiitake stems (or compost them along with what's left in the strainer like the responsible global citizen you are). Slice the shiitake caps and set aside.

**3** Measure out your strained broth. If you have less than 4½ cups of it, top the rest off with water. Return the broth to the pot and stir in the cooked rice. Bring to a gentle simmer and cook, stirring occasionally but not obsessively, until it turns to porridge, about 15 minutes. (You could stop at this point and throw the porridge in the fridge, then bring it all together in the morning for a killer boil-and-serve breakfast—just bring it back to a simmer before proceeding.) Stir in the corn kernels and simmer until they are cooked, 3 to 5 minutes. Stir in the miso and butter and remove from the heat.

**4** Serve in bowls topped with the sliced shiitakes, sliced scallion greens, and a drizzle of soy sauce or black vinegar to taste.

# MUSHROOM MAPO TOFU

Looking back, I could cleave my life into two halves: the time before I knew mapo tofu and the time after. It is absolutely one of my favorite foods and I thought that because there's so much delicious gunk in it, swapping out the small amount of meat in the traditional dish for something else would be easy peasy. Not true! I'm happy with this cruelty-free rendition we arrived at, but be warned that unlike take-out mapo, it's not just as good the next day. You wanna take it down hot.

**MAKES 4 SERVINGS**

| | |
|---|---|
| **1 oz** | dried shiitake mushrooms, soaked in 4 C water for at least 30 minutes |
| **5 oz** | fresh shiitake or button mushrooms |
| **+** | kosher salt |
| **1 lb** | soft tofu, cut into 1″ cubes |
| **2 T** | neutral oil |
| **1** | leek, halved lengthwise and sliced into 1″ pieces on an angle |
| **1 T** | chopped garlic |
| **1 T** | chopped fresh ginger |
| **2 T** | doubanjiang |
| **2 T** | spicy chili crisp |
| **1 T** | black bean paste (very optional but nice) |
| **2 t** | coarsely ground Sichuan peppercorns |
| **1 t** | gochugaru |
| **1 T** | cornstarch mixed with 1 T cold water to form a slurry |
| **+** | cooked jasmine rice, for serving |

**1** Remove the shiitakes from their soaking liquid but keep that liquid near at hand. Finely chop the fresh and dried mushrooms with a cleaver, knife, or mechanical food chopper of some sort.

**2** Bring a medium pot of water to the boil and salt it. Have all your mise en place readied and measured and near the stove.

**3** Add the tofu cubes and poach them for 2 to 3 minutes. Drain, season with salt, and keep warm.

**4** Heat 1 tablespoon of the oil in a wok (or large, deep skillet, but, *come on*, get a wok!) over high heat. Add the mushrooms and cook, scraping from underneath the mushrooms and folding them over, arranging them in a thin layer around the wok, until they release their liquid and it evaporates, about 8 minutes. Add the leek, garlic, and ginger and stir-fry for 3 minutes. Scoop the vegetables onto a plate and wipe out the wok.

**5** Add the remaining 1 tablespoon oil to the wok and put it back over high heat. Add the *doubanjiang*, chili crisp, black bean paste (if using), Sichuan pepper, and *gochugaru* and stir to combine. Fry them, stirring so they do not burn, until the oil separates from the mixture, about 1 minute. Stir the mushroom soaking liquid into the fiery stuff in the wok, then add back the stir-fried vegetables to the mixture and bring to a boil. Stir in the cornstarch slurry and boil again. Stir in the tofu cubes, coating them in the mapo stew. Serve with rice, hot.

# SICHUAN SQUASH STEW

This is a version of a smart dish Danny Bowien serves at Mission Chinese Food—he makes his with sweet potato greens instead of watercress, and works a little bit harder on building up the umami in his broth. This is the night-school-at-a-community-college version of his dish, with easier-to-find ingredients and almost all of the punch. It is a warming, filling soup that's got all the character of the sort of psychedelic Sichuan food that he's known for but also a healthful/restorative/I-just-finished-yoga-and-feel-good-eating-this quality that might mean it ends up on your dinner table more often than you suspect looking at it here on the page.

**MAKES 4 SERVINGS**

| | |
|---|---|
| ¼ C | dried adzuki beans |
| + | kosher salt |
| 1 lb | kabocha squash, cut into 1″ wedges |
| 3 T | extra-virgin olive oil |
| 1 | dried shiitake mushroom |
| 1 t | chopped garlic |
| 2 T | sambal oelek, plus more for garnish |
| + | fish sauce (optional) |
| 8 oz | watercress cut into 2″ pieces |
| 2 T | pumpkin seeds |

**1** Combine the adzuki beans with enough water to cover by 3 inches in a large saucepan and bring to a boil. Reduce the heat and simmer until the beans are tender, about 45 minutes. Add 1 teaspoon salt to the water and let the beans cool.

**2** Meanwhile, heat the oven to 350°F. Rub the squash with 1 tablespoon of the olive oil and arrange in a roasting pan. Roast the squash until tender and a little caramelized, about 1 hour. Let cool, then remove the skin. Cut half of the wedges into bite-size chunks. Purée the remaining squash with ½ cup of water.

**3** Buzz the shiitake in a spice grinder to make mushroom powder. Reserve. (If you're not inclined to blitz a dried mushroom to make a soup, throw a few dried shiitakes in with the 3 cups of water you'll be adding in the next step and boil up a rich-tasting/smelling mushroom broth. Why not throw a piece of kombu in there too if you have it?)

**4** Drain the adzuki beans and pat dry. Heat a wok over medium-high heat and when the wok emits a wisp of smoke, add the remaining 2 tablespoons oil. The oil should immediately ripple. Add the garlic, adzuki beans, and mushroom powder. Add 3 cups of water, the sambal, and squash purée. Bring to a simmer and cook for 5 minutes for the flavors to meld. Fold the squash chunks into the stew and simmer 1 minute to warm through. Season with salt and a few dashes of fish sauce, if desired. Add the watercress and remove from the heat.

**5** Ladle into bowls and garnish with the pumpkin seeds and additional sambal, if desired.

# PAPPA AL POMODORO

Did you ever eat English muffin pizzas as an after-school snack? They are delightful, a high achievement in toaster-oven cuisine.

When we were examining *pappa al pomodoro* for inclusion in this distinguished compendium, we liked it—but it wasn't quite powerful enough. But eating it reminded me of a years-ago conversation with the chef Mario Carbone, in which he told me about making a canapé in which English muffin pizzas drown in tomato sauce, *pappa*-style.

Having never seen that dish, nor having any use for canapés on a regular basis, I offer you this debased derivative: pappa al pomodoro al toaster-oven pizzaiolo. If normalcy is more of what you want to see, substitute a rustico loaf for the English muffins and dial down or eliminate the oregano, and you'll be back under the Tuscan sun instead of sitting in the glare of after-school cartoons.

**MAKES 4 SERVINGS**

| | |
|---|---|
| **4** | English muffins |
| **¼ C** | extra-virgin olive oil, plus more for drizzling |
| **2** | garlic cloves, chopped |
| **½ C** | chopped basil, plus basil chiffonade for garnish |
| **1 t** | dried oregano |
| **1 t** | kosher salt |
| **½ t** | chili flakes |
| **1** | can (28 oz) whole peeled tomatoes |
| **+** | grated cheese or chili flakes—any of your favorite pizza condiments are welcome |

**1** Fork-split the English muffins. Toast them in a toaster or 450°F oven until they are dark brown and dried out. Let cool.

**2** Heat the olive oil in a large saucepan or small soup pot. Add the garlic and fry until the garlic is soft, about 2 minutes. Stir in the chopped basil, oregano, salt, and chili flakes, then add the tomatoes. Break up the tomatoes with a wooden spoon, then add a half can of water to the pot. Bring to a simmer and cook, uncovered, for 15 minutes.

**3** Break up the English muffins into 1-inch pieces and toss into the tomato sauce. Fold the muffin bits to coat in the sauce and simmer for about 5 minutes, until the soup thickens. Turn off the heat and let the *pappa* stand 15 minutes.

**4** Serve at room temperature, drizzled with olive oil and scattered with basil. Garnish with your favorite pizza toppings.

#814

# VICHYSSOISE

I know what you're thinking. *Really?? Vichyssoise? What is this, 1973?* And yes, every vaguely continental cookbook with nicotine-stained pages from a used bookstore will have an entry on this soup. Why? Because EASE IS POWER. And how many cold soups satisfy like this one? None. Also: We make ours with dashi. Heap it with caviar or chopped tomato or any kind of chilled protein to make a proper uptown-lady luncheon course out of it. Drink it straight from the fridge when no one's looking if you're like me.

**MAKES 4 SERVINGS**

- **3** large leeks, white and palest green parts only
- **4 T** unsalted butter
- **1 lb** russet potatoes, peeled and chopped
- **5 C** broth (see note)
- **+** kosher salt
- **½ C** half-and-half
- **+** freshly ground black pepper

**Note on broth:** We've made this every which way. Water makes a meager soup. A vegetable broth like the one on page 128 does a good, classic job. But for the fully powered approach, we like dashi: You can make a kombu dashi by steeping a few pieces of kombu in 5 cups of water overnight or steeping them together in a pan over low heat for 20 to 40 minutes. Or just dissolve 2 teaspoons of hondashi (instant dashi) in the water and call it a day!

**1** Halve the leeks lengthwise and rinse them, inside and out, under cool running water. Leeks are always so sandy! Why? If your leeks aren't sandy, you might be happy, but where were they grown? The sand is the earth's way of saying I MADE THAT. Still, it must be washed away for the soup to be made. Thank you, Earth. Pat the leeks dry and thinly slice crosswise.

**2** Melt the butter in a large saucepan over medium heat and add the leeks. Stir to coat them in the fat and cook them, stirring often, until they've softened but not taken on any color, about 8 minutes.

**3** Add the potatoes, broth, and 2 teaspoons salt. Bring to a simmer and cook until the potatoes are tender, about 30 minutes. Remove from the heat and cool slightly.

**4** Blend the soup, in batches if necessary, until very smooth. Chill the soup for at least 4 hours, and preferably overnight. Stir in the half-and-half. Taste the soup and reseason with salt and pepper. Garnish as you like. A dollop of crème fraîche and a healthy scattering of chopped chives is nice.

# CARROTS IN CARROT DASHI

A Dave Chang classic, though it's more or less stolen from Mauro Colagreco, who cooks at Mirazur outside of Nice, in the extra pretty coastal part of France.

Juice carrots fresh for this dish or buy carrot juice fresh from some kinda health food place where all the models go. If you don't have a place like that near your house yet, wait between six months and fifteen years. New York is so lousy with juice bars I'm sure we'll start exporting them everywhere soon. And truth be told even the fresh bottled carrot juice that industrial carrot slaughterer Bolthouse Farms sells these days works well.

■ ▬ ▬▬ ▬▬▬▬▬▬▬▬▬▬▬▬▬▬▬▬▬▬▬▬▬▬▬▬

**MAKES 2 SERVINGS**

- **1 C**  carrot juice
- **1**  sheet kombu
- **2 T**  unsalted butter
- **4**  carrots, scrubbed
- **+**  kosher salt (Maldon salt if you're feeling fancy)

**Note:** This recipe is the most up-to-date and, frankly, resolutely delicious version of this dish, but the end results are very straightforward looking: It is a dish of carrots in carrot juice. So we decided to re-create the peacocky original for the photo: Some of the carrots have been browned in butter before being cooked in dashi; purple carrots have been shaved and pickled into exotically colorful garnishes; some of the carrots have been puréed into a mush to anchor the carrots on the plate; even the carrot tops make an appearance. If any of that frippery appeals to you, by all means, get to work. None of it's bad. But EASE IS POWER forever and ever amen.

**1** Combine the carrot juice and kombu in a saucepan and heat together over your stove's lowest heat. If you've got 20 to 40 minutes to let the seaweed steep in the juice, excellent. Less time is also okay. If you wanted to be a really cold-brew yoga snob, you could put the kombu in the carrot juice overnight in the fridge for a long no-temperature extraction. Namaste.

**2** Melt the butter in a high-sided pan over medium heat. Once the butter foam subsides, add the carrots and a large pinch of salt. Toss once to coat the carrots in the butter and add the carrot juice, discarding the kombu. Cover the pan and cook, shaking it or opening the lid to stir the carrots occasionally. Gauge the doneness of the carrots after 6 or 7 minutes, and cook them to your taste—al dente or left-my-dentures-on-the-nightstand soft. Serve as is. A scattering of Maldon salt is as much as it might want.

# RIBOLLITA

This is New York chef Marco Canora's ribollita recipe, which is the best ribollita we know. A few things: Until you add a cheese-topped toast at the last minute, this is vegan, and as a vegan stew-soup, it is nearly unbeatable; also, you should stop eating all your kale raw and try it out in a setting like this where it can really shine. Finally, you will make this soup in this quantity and not reduce it because it can be reheated again and again without any negative impact on its quality (it is "re-boiled" in name, after all) and because you will rue not having extra around if you don't.

■■ ■■ ■■■ ■■

**MAKES 1 GALLON (8 SERVINGS)**

| | |
|---|---|
| **2 T** | extra-virgin olive oil, plus more for drizzling |
| **3 C** | diced onions |
| **3 C** | diced carrots |
| **3 C** | diced celery |
| **+** | kosher salt |
| **4 C** | chopped savoy cabbage (about ½ head) |
| **⅓ C** | tomato paste |
| **8 C** | chopped dinosaur kale (about 2 bunches) |
| **10 C** | water |
| **5 C** | cooked cannellini beans (or use canned like we did, but don't tell Marco!) |
| **+** | freshly ground black pepper |
| **+** | thin slices of bread, toasted |
| **+** | freshly grated Parmigiano-Reggiano cheese |
| **+** | fresh thyme leaves |

**1** Heat the olive oil in a large pot over medium heat. Add the onions, carrots, and celery. Season with salt and stir to coat the vegetables with oil. Cover and sweat the vegetables, stirring occasionally, until they begin to soften, about 10 minutes.

**2** Add the savoy cabbage and mix well. Cover and cook until it begins to wilt, about 3 minutes.

**3** Stir in the tomato paste, taking care to distribute it evenly. Reduce the heat to low and add the kale. Mix well, cover the pot, and stew the vegetables until they are tender, about 20 minutes. Add 8 cups of the water, increase the heat, and bring the soup to a boil.

**4** Meanwhile, purée 3 cups of the beans and the remaining 2 cups water in a blender or food processor, adding a little water if necessary.

**5** Whisk the purée into the soup and add the remaining 2 cups beans. Bring the soup back to a boil, then reduce the heat and gently simmer, uncovered, until the flavors meld, about 30 minutes.

**6** Season the soup with salt and lots of pepper. At this point, the soup can be cooled and refrigerated or frozen. To serve, ladle the hot soup into bowls. Top each serving with toast, Parmigiano, pepper, thyme leaves, and a drizzle of oil.

# *VIGNAROLA*

*Vignarola* comes from Rome, and comes to this book from our Italian photographer, Gabriele. He says that vignarola translates to "vineyard greens," but because it's composed of greens that only come up in the springtime, when the vineyards are basically dead, it's more likely an invocation of the greengrocer, who was, in olden times, called a *vignarolo*.

Of course the Americans have debased it further: Rather than cooking all the vegetables individually like *nonna* would have, we make it as a one-pot dish. And even though we have *amore* for the greengrocer, we find that frozen fava beans (sold at Indian and Italian markets and sometimes Whole Foods) work just fine and can even be swapped out for edamame if that's all you can score.

If you have a lifestyle that allows a little pig to play in the vegetable patch, seek out guanciale when you make vignarola—and know that the dish works just fine without it.

**MAKES 4 MAIN-COURSE SERVINGS**

| | |
|---|---|
| **2 oz** | guanciale, cut into ¼" pieces (optional) |
| **4 T** | olive oil |
| **3** | garlic cloves, peeled |
| **8** | baby artichokes or 4 medium artichokes, cleaned and cut into ½" wedges |
| **1** | small onion, finely chopped |
| **1½ C** | shucked fresh fava beans (from 1½ lb in the pod) or thawed frozen |
| **1½ C** | peas, thawed if frozen |
| **2–3 C** | vegetable stock or water |
| **+** | kosher salt |
| **4 T** | unsalted butter |
| **¼ C** | packed fresh mint leaves |
| **1 C** | thinly sliced romaine or butter lettuce |

**1** If using the guanciale, blanch it in a small pot of simmering water for 1 minute. Drain and reserve.

**2** Heat 2 tablespoons of the olive oil and the garlic cloves in a wide Dutch oven or deep cast iron skillet over medium heat. Let the garlic sizzle until golden, about 3 minutes. Remove with a slotted spoon and discard. Add the artichokes to the pot, in batches if necessary, and brown them, flipping to caramelize all sides, about 8 minutes. Transfer the artichokes to a plate.

**3** Add the remaining 2 tablespoons oil to the pot and stir in the onion. After 2 minutes, when the onion is sizzling and translucent around the edges, stir in the blanched guanciale. Continue cooking until the onion and pork are browned and the guanciale is rendered, about 8 minutes longer.

**4** Stir in the favas and peas. If the beans are fresh, roll them around in the onion and fat for a few minutes to get them cooking. If they were previously frozen, simply stir into the onion-pig mix along with the artichokes. When everything sizzles, pour in the stock so the vegetables are in a deep puddle but not quite submerged. Season with salt and bring to a simmer. Partially cover the stew and let it bubble for 5 to 10 minutes, until the artichokes and favas are tender. Stir in the butter and adjust the seasoning with salt as necessary. Remove from the heat and fold in the mint and lettuce. Serve warm with bread for sopping.

# ENSEMBLE PLAYERS

# BRAISED DAIKON WITH MUSTARD

A big radish. A subtle power.

Boiling the tuber in the rice-washing water supposedly extracts its bitterness. Simmering it in the sweet, salty, umami-rich liquid supposedly makes it taste delicious. Pickled mustard seeds supposedly go with just about everything, at least according to the person writing this book.

The mysteries of this dish are yours to revel in and explore.

**MAKES 2 TO 4 SERVINGS**

| | |
|---|---|
| **1 or 2** | large daikon radishes (about 1½ lb) |
| **1 t** | kosher salt, plus a pinch |
| **+** | rice-washing water |
| **3 T** | soy sauce |
| **2 T** | mirin |
| **1 T** | hondashi |
| **1 T** | sugar |
| **+** | Pickled Mustard Seeds (recipe follows) or prepared Japanese mustard, for serving |

**1** Peel the daikon and cut them into 1-inch-thick disks. Bevel the edges of the disks and mark them with an X on both sides. (Why? A hard 90-degree-angle edge will fray in long cooking and look less beautiful than the beveled one. The X makes cutting the pieces of daikon with chopsticks much easier.)

**2** Combine the prepared daikon, a pinch of salt, and the rice-washing water to cover in a sauce pot and bring to a boil over high heat. (If you aren't cooking rice, you can put 3 tablespoons of unwashed raw rice in a tea bag or tea strainer and put it in a pot with the daikon and water to cover.) Reduce the heat and simmer for 10 minutes. Drain the daikon (discard the cooking water) and return it to the pot.

**3** Add 3½ cups water, 1 teaspoon salt, the soy sauce, mirin, hondashi, and sugar. Bring to a gentle simmer over medium heat and cook until very tender but not falling apart, about 30 minutes. Store in the cooking liquid until ready to eat, then serve with something mustardy, hot or warm or cold, depending on the season and the setting.

## PICKLED MUSTARD SEEDS

**MAKES 1 CUP**

| | |
|---|---|
| **¾ C** | white wine vinegar |
| **¾ C** | water |
| **¼ C** | sugar |
| **1½ t** | kosher salt |
| **½ C** | yellow mustard seeds |

Combine the vinegar, water, sugar, salt, and mustard seeds in a saucepan and bring to a simmer. Simmer gently, uncovered, until the liquid is reduced by half, 45 minutes; the seeds should swell to look like little caviar pearls. Cool and reserve in the remaining liquid. These keep in the refrigerator forever.

# ASPARAGUS LIKE A STEAK

There is much talk in professional kitchens of learning how to cook meat, and while there is much to learn about the proper manipulation of flesh, the thing most people (in the European tradition) are talking about is this: browning it over high heat, mellowing it out, then basting it in an endless cascade of herb-scented butter until it's at the appropriate level of doneness. There are few meats that don't show well treated like that. And, frankly, it works on lots of vegetables too. The two I think of most often are carrots and asparagus, both of which take on color and play well with butter.

**MAKES 4 SERVINGS**

| | |
|---|---|
| **2 T** | neutral oil |
| **2 lb** | fat green or white asparagus spears |
| **4 T** | unsalted butter, cut into 1 T pieces, chilled |
| **4** | garlic cloves |
| **1** | handful thyme sprigs |
| **+** | flaky sea salt |
| **+** | lemon wedges, for serving |

**1** Heat a large cast iron skillet over high heat until a wisp of smoke rises from the surface. Add the oil, let it come to temperature for 30 seconds, then add about half of the asparagus—there should be a spear's width of free space between each piece.

**2** Let the asparagus brown, cooking unmolested, 1 to 2 minutes. Shake the pan to roll them around, then add 2 tablespoons of the butter, 2 of the garlic cloves, and half of the thyme. Tilt the pan toward you and use a large spoon to scoop the melting butter up and over the asparagus, basting it in hot fat. Baste the asparagus until they and the butter are nicely browned, about 2 minutes. Lift the asparagus from the pan and arrange on a warm platter. Pour over the browned butter, then wipe out the skillet and repeat with the remaining asparagus, butter, garlic, and thyme until you have filled a large platter.

**3** Sprinkle the asparagus liberally with flaky sea salt and serve with lemon wedges.

# BBQ CARROTS WITH HOMEMADE RANCH

Marc Vetri is one of America's most masterful masters of authentic Italian cuisine. But here, he shows off his ability to put the CLASS in TRASH instead. Okay, admittedly, he makes his own barbecue sauce and I'm telling you to buy KC Masterpiece (or another similar/preferred bottled sauce) because I'm pro-ease.

*Why not buy the ranch too?* you might be asking. Because Vetri's ranch is a wonderful extra-ranchy ranch that's worth the effort. Of course if you don't listen to me on that point and sneak off into the Hidden Valley I'll probably never know unless I'm hiding in your house somewhere observing every tiny creepy little detail of your life and keeping careful note of how often you trim your toenails.

But the payoff isn't about class or toenails or Italia, it's about the versatility of carrots, and the pleasure of a dish that reconfigures the experience of eating carrots dipped in ranch at a backyard cookout into a fun-to-eat side dish. Squiggle the ranch over the carrots if it appeals; we opted to put it in a dipping bowl here.

**MAKES 4 SERVINGS**

- **2 lb** medium carrots
- **2 T** extra-virgin olive oil
- **+** kosher salt and freshly ground black pepper
- **½ C** archetypal supermarket barbecue sauce
- **+** Ranch Dressing (recipe follows)

**1** Heat a charcoal or gas grill to medium or the broiler to high.

**2** Wash and trim the carrots, then halve them lengthwise. Toss the carrots with the olive oil, salt and pepper to taste, and half of the barbecue sauce—add more if needed; they should be glazed in it. Grill or broil the carrots, turning and basting with more sauce, until they are nicely charred but not burned, 5 or 6 minutes. Move to a cooler spot on the grill or turn the oven down to 350°F, and continue cooking the carrots until tender but not mushy (you can test them with a thin knife or a fork; they should yield but not mush), about 10 minutes in total.

**3** Serve the carrots with the ranch drizzled all over the place or chastely segregated in its own bowl.

## RANCH DRESSING
**MAKES ABOUT ½ CUP**

- **1½ T** dried parsley
- **½ t** dried dill
- **½ t** garlic powder
- **½ t** onion powder
- **¼ t** dried chives
- **¼ t** kosher salt
- **¼ t** freshly ground black pepper
- **⅛ t** cayenne pepper
- **¼ C** mayonnaise
- **¼ C** buttermilk, plus more if desired

**1** Combine the dried herbs and spices in a spice or coffee grinder and blitz them into a green powder. (Don't have the power tools? Don't worry. Just stir 'em together.)

**2** In a bowl, stir together the mayonnaise, buttermilk, and green herb/spice powder. Thin with additional buttermilk as you see fit. This will keep for days in the refrigerator, good in all the places that ranch usually is.

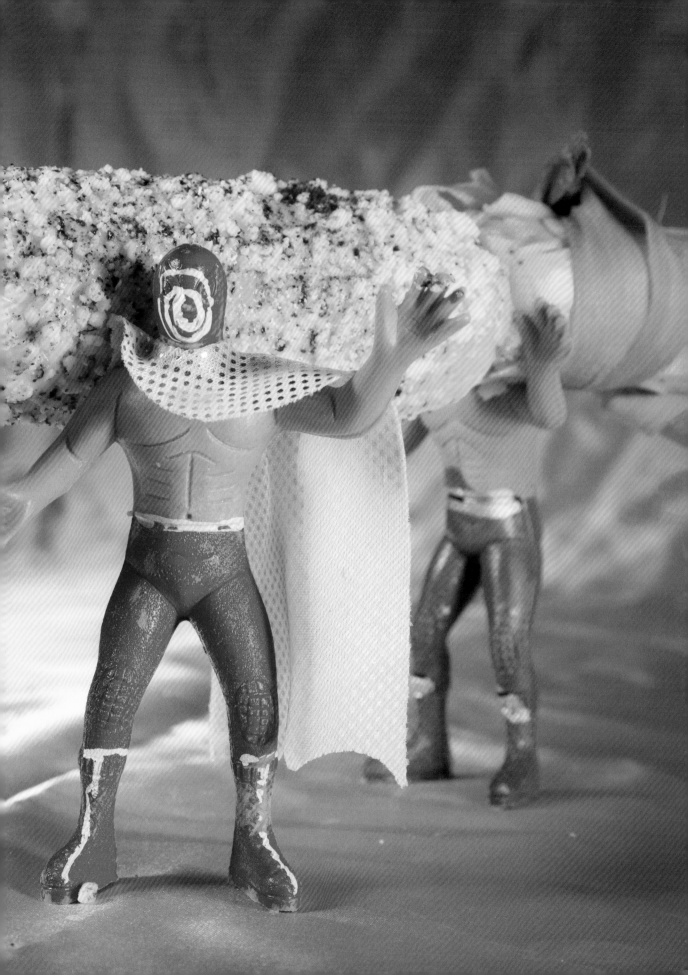

# ELOTE

The great thing about *elotes* is how little there is to them. To describe the dish is to give the recipe for it: grilled corn slathered with mayo and cheese, spiked with chili powder and lime. But ease is not the seat of the elote's power, flavor is: sweet corn, salty cheese, unctuous mayo, caliente chili powder, lime zing! Plus it comes on its own stick. Elotes are the total package.

**MAKES 4 SERVINGS**

| | |
|---|---|
| **4** | ears corn |
| **¼ C** | mayonnaise |
| **½ C** | crumbled cotija cheese or finely grated parmesan cheese |
| **1 t** | chili powder |
| **+** | lime wedges |

**1** Pull back the corn husks and remove the silk. Remove a few strips of husk and use them to tie the remaining attached husk around the end of each cob, forming a handle.

**2** To roast the corn, heat a grill or broiler to medium-high. (You can also char the corn over a gas burner.) Set the corn over or under the flames and roast until it crackles and pops. Turn frequently, charring the corn evenly, for 7 to 8 minutes.

**3** Immediately brush the corn with the mayonnaise (it is nice if you apply it with a brush, though the back of a spoon works A-okay too) and sprinkle with the cheese and chili powder. Serve with lime wedges and do not let your friends dig in until they've given their cobs a squirt.

# GOMEN WAT

*Gomen wat* is Ethiopian alchemy at its finest: spices that are beguiling but not overwhelming, collards sublimated by butter, their minerality giving over to the whole. I find that a pot of these collards and a few slices of rye sourdough (rye having a similar tang to *injera,* the teff-based flatbread you'd eat with gomen wat in an Ethiopian setting) make for a great meal. I also stumbled into the realization that gomen wat makes a good pasta sauce: I was cleaning up from a weekend lunch that included gomen wat for adults and buttered cartwheel pasta for my daughters and started snacking while I was washing dishes.

**MAKES 2 TO 4 SERVINGS**

| | |
|---|---|
| **1 t** | coriander seeds |
| **1 t** | cumin seeds |
| **½ t** | black cardamom seeds (from 2–3 pods) |
| **½ t** | fenugreek seeds |
| **2 T** | butter |
| **1** | small onion, chopped |
| **1 T** | minced garlic |
| **2 T** | minced fresh ginger (from a 2″ piece) |
| **1** | jalapeño chili, seeded and chopped |
| **2 C** | water |
| **1 lb** | collard greens (1 large bunch), stemmed and very thinly sliced |
| **+** | kosher salt |

**1** Toast the coriander, cumin, cardamom, and fenugreek seeds in a large skillet over medium-low heat until aromatic, about 1 minute. Add the butter to the skillet and stir until the foam subsides. Add the onion and sweat until soft, about 8 minutes. Add the garlic, ginger, and jalapeño and continue sweating for 2 to 3 minutes. Add the water, bring to a boil, and cook until reduced by one-third. Carefully transfer to a blender and process the aromatic broth until smooth. If cooking the collards immediately, return the broth to the skillet. If cooking later, cool and refrigerate the broth for up to 3 days.

**2** Bring the broth to a simmer and add the collards. Once they wilt, season with salt and partially cover the skillet. Simmer the greens gently until tender, about 40 minutes.

# BROOKS HEADLEY AND JULIA GOLDBERG

## SUPERIORITY BURGER, NYC

**PM:** How do you approach making vegetables POWERFUL here at Superiority Burger?

**BH:** I like to do dramatic readings of this one vegetarian restaurant's Instagram feed before service, because everything they make has like fifty-five ingredients and there's always green beans. That's not how we do it. But to answer your question: a lot of different ways, I guess. Julia, sometimes you just come with the fully formed idea.

**JG:** I always think about what's good right now, like what we can get. In the winter it's important to try not to do something with something like green beans—unless it's consciously using frozen green beans to make green bean casserole, which I love.

**BH:** We have a lot of people come with dietary eliminations here. So, there are some things we'll intentionally make vegan or gluten-free. But sometimes, it's not intentional. I'm addicted to bread and pretzels—when I snack, that's what I go for without even thinking about it. So when we were working on this sweet-potato dish, I said, "Throw some bread crumbs on it" to make it crunchy, to give it texture. And Julia was like, *We're not putting any bread on this.*

I stormed off like a petulant little kid: "Well, it's not gonna be any good." And then her idea was this potato with a bunch of stuff on it, including chopped-up pickles for crunch. And I was like, *Pshhh, whatever*. But it works perfectly—and it wasn't necessarily like we were trying to make a gluten-free side. It was more like, she's had enough of me putting bread on things.

**JG:** I guess I spend a lot of time thinking about a recipe before I even start playing with it. I grew up with Midwestern parents who didn't cook for me ever, so I ate a lot of Mahatma and Zatarain's beans and rice—which were mainly salt bombs that I'd make better by adding margarine.

And now I approach something like, how can I make a vegetable dish as satisfying and hit all the points of perfectly processed food, without being processed? How can I get the sweet and the salty and the crunchy and the sour? Like that feeling when you eat a Dorito and you're like *Agh, this has everything I could ever want.*

**BH:** Julia is also good at figuring out how to make things taste trashy enough that you feel like you're eating something kind of bad for you—even when it's a creamy vegan dressing on shredded kohlrabi and kohlrabi stumps.

I can always tell when we're tasting whatever is new, I'll be like "Oh it's just not there yet; it's too austere at this point." And that could be with high levels of salt and acid and char. Usually it's just like one little twist, and it's not usually adding an element. It's more like taking it away to make it like . . . like a Dorito.

**JG:** Right now, I'm just starting this collards dish. I really like braised greens, and I worked for Anna Klinger [the chef of Al di Là trattoria and Lincoln Station, both in Brooklyn] who would cook greens with some garlic, chili flakes, and parm broth, and serve it with white bean purée. That's what she always does; that's like, her thing. I wanted to do a braised green that wasn't kale, and I thought collards would be great—and I wanted to make it creamy, almost creamed. Then I was like, *Oh, maybe peanut butter would work.*

**PM:** That's like Senegalese food.

**BH:** None of what we serve is claiming in any way to be directly authentic to anything. Maybe that's a place that you're coming from, but the end result doesn't taste West African, even though it's got those ingredients in it. We were going to put sweet potatoes in it, but then we were like, we put sweet potatoes in everything.

**JG:** And also that makes it even more Southern or puts it in some kind of category, which I don't like to do. I'm kind of a picky eater, and my dad is the most picky eater, so I always think, *Would he try this? Would he eat this?*

**BH:** Since we're closed on Tuesdays Julia and I will go around to different places. At the end of the year, we went on kind of a salad thing, where we would go to fancy restaurants and sit at the bar and just order salads, just to see what other people were doing. A lot of the time, they were too

austere. Maybe they were even with the same stuff as ours, the same ingredients that we were using, but they weren't gut-level satisfying. There's no reason a shredded raw vegetable can't be as satisfying as a cheeseburger. . . . Because it can be. There's no reason it shouldn't be.

**PM:** Are there ingredients in your larder that you reach for *for power*?

**BH:** I went to Kalustyan's [a sprawling Indian grocery store in Manhattan] and, as usual, I couldn't spend less than like two hundred dollars. There's so much stuff there you can use, and not necessarily to make Indian food.

**JG:** We're not heavy on anything in particular, but a lot of vegan and vegetarian cooks have their three ingredients that they'll use a lot, like nutritional yeast or amino acids.

**BH:** We buy a lot of vinegar. I feel like we spend a lot of money on fermented liquid.

**PM:** Is acid something vegetables need more of than people give to it?

**BH:** Yeah. Which is counterintuitive, because salad dressing is ostensibly acid. But it is rarely acid *enough*.

**JG:** I think salt too. You don't realize how salty salad dressing is because it's always on salad, so when you make it yourself and you're tasting it, it's almost like you have to make it *too* salty. I think it's also about taking things far enough. Like with the cucumber salad in the summer, charring the scallions gave it that little extra boost. And also making sure that when we toast nuts, we toast them dark enough.

**BH:** Maybe we even take some of the elements too far to eat straight, but they are good when consumed as part of the whole. Often, taking certain elements way too far to eat on their own works when you put them back together as the whole.

# JULIA'S BRAISED COLLARDS WITH PEANUT BUTTER

Read about the genesis of this dish in the previous pages. Cook it because the combo sounds killer, or cook it because you can't wrap your head around it. The results will be the same: membership in the clean plate club, and an extended appreciation for how good collards can be.

**MAKES 4 SERVINGS**

| | |
|---|---|
| **2 T** | neutral oil |
| **2** | yellow onions, finely diced |
| **+** | kosher salt |
| **1–2** | chili peppers, like habanero or Fresno, sliced into rings or half-moons |
| **2** | garlic cloves, thinly sliced |
| **2 T** | tomato paste |
| **2 T** | apple cider vinegar |
| **2 lb** | collard greens, stemmed and torn into 2" pieces |
| **3 C** | water |
| **½ C** | peanut butter |
| **+** | freshly ground black pepper |
| **2** | thick slices sourdough bread |
| **+** | Hot Honey (recipe follows) |
| **½ C** | roasted peanuts |

**1** Heat the oil in a large, heavy pot over medium-high heat. Add the onions, season with salt, and cook, stirring occasionally, until the onions pick up some color, about 5 minutes. Reduce the heat and continue cooking until the onions are totally soft, about 20 minutes.

**2** Add the sliced chili and cook for a couple of minutes to soften. Add the garlic and cook a few minutes more until it starts to soften. Stir in the tomato paste, coating the vegetables with it, and cook until it darkens a few shades, 3 to 4 minutes. Add the cider vinegar and use it to help scrape up browned bits from the bottom of the pot.

**3** Add the collards, a handful at a time, wilting them between additions. Pour 2 cups of the water into the pot, season with a pinch of salt, cover, and simmer the greens for 10 minutes.

**4** Uncover the pot and stir. Add the peanut butter and swirl until it dissolves into the pot liquor. Add the remaining 1 cup water to the pot, cover, and simmer the greens until they are tender, about 30 minutes longer. Season with salt, if needed, and pepper. At this point the collards can be cooled and refrigerated up to 3 days.

**5** When ready to serve, warm the collards. Grill or toast slices of sourdough bread until charred. Break into large bites and place in the bottom of shallow bowls. Spoon the collards and juices over the bread and drizzle with the hot honey. Sprinkle with the peanuts and serve.

## HOT HONEY

It's halfway to silly to break this out as a recipe, but I'm doing it to remind you how delicious hot honey is to add to, you know, foods in general, and that it's simpler than a sneeze to "make."

**MAKES ¼ CUP**

| | |
|---|---|
| **2 T** | Frank's RedHot sauce |
| **2 T** | honey |
| **+** | kosher salt |
| **+** | freshly ground black pepper |

Make the honey hot: Stir the hot sauce and honey in a small bowl until smooth. Season with a pinch each of salt and pepper. Reserve for serving.

# ROASTED VEGETABLES WITH FISH SAUCE VINAIGRETTE

This dish is our Helen of Troy: the one that launched a hundred power vegetables. It can be made with a mix of vegetables, as it is here, or just one vegetable, the way they do it at Momofuku Ssam Bar. Power awaits you on whichever path you choose.

■ ■■ ■■■ ■

**MAKES 4 SERVINGS**

- **¾ lb** Brussels sprouts, halved
- **¾ lb** cauliflower (1 small head), broken into 1–2″ florets
- **¾ lb** carrots (4–5 medium), cut into 1–2″ pieces
- **2 T** grapeseed oil
- **+** Fish Sauce Vinaigrette (recipe follows)
- **1 T** very thinly sliced cilantro stems, plus ¼ C cilantro leaves
- **2 T** chopped fresh mint

**1** Heat the oven to 425°F.

**2** Toss the Brussels sprouts, cauliflower, and carrots with the grapeseed oil in a bowl, then dump onto one or two rimmed baking sheets. Wipe out the bowl and keep it handy. If you have the patience, turn the vegetables so their flat cut sides are touching the pan to ensure maximum caramelization. Make sure the vegetables have a little room to breathe and aren't layered on top of one another. This will help them crisp and brown instead of getting all steamed and soggy.

**3** Roast the vegetables until they are charred in spots and tender but not soft, about 25 minutes.

**4** Toss the hot vegetables in the bowl with the fish sauce vinaigrette, cilantro, and mint. Serve.

## FISH SAUCE VINAIGRETTE

**MAKES ABOUT ½ CUP**

- **¼ C** fish sauce
- **¼ C** water
- **2 T** rice vinegar
- **2 T** fresh lime juice
- **¼ C** sugar
- **1** garlic clove, minced
- **3** fresh red bird's-eye chilies, thinly sliced, seeds intact, or 1 t chili paste, such as sambal oelek

Combine the fish sauce, water, vinegar, lime juice, sugar, garlic, and chilies in a bowl and stir to dissolve the sugar.

# KADDU

*Kaddu* is a brilliant and simple way to make pumpkin (or butternut squash, as we call for here, or really any of those orange 'n' starchy things that pop up in the market around Halloween) a worthy main course. The finished dish—which wouldn't be surprising to find on any North Indian table, though my coworker Priya Krishna's mom, who gave me the recipe, serves it on Thanksgiving alongside all the pilgrim's fare—should be hot, sweet, sour, and salty all at once. Priya tells me this dish is best eaten with hot puri, a deep-fried Indian bread, but I've had it with plain old basmati rice and/or naan (see page 210) and been happy all the same.

**MAKES 4 SERVINGS**

| | |
|---|---|
| **2 T** | olive oil |
| **1 t** | fenugreek seeds |
| **½ t** | ground turmeric |
| **1** | small onion, diced |
| **½ t** | chili powder or ¼ t cayenne pepper |
| **¼ t** | hing (optional but real nice) |
| **1** | piece (2") fresh ginger, peeled and julienned (about 2 T) |
| **1** | 2 lb butternut squash, peeled and cut into ¾" cubes |
| **+** | kosher salt |
| **1 lb** | plum tomatoes, cut into medium dice |
| **2 T** | fresh lime juice |
| **2 T** | light brown sugar |
| **2 T** | chopped cilantro |

**1** Warm a large, deep skillet over medium heat and add the olive oil. When it shimmers, add the fenugreek seeds. They should splatter as they hit the oil. Reduce the heat and add the turmeric, swirling it into the oil. Add the onion and cook just until it starts to soften, 3 to 4 minutes. Stir in the chili powder, asafetida (if using), and ginger. Cook for 1 minute and then add the butternut squash and toss to coat the squash in the contents of the pan. Season with a large pinch of salt, cover, and let the squash steam until just fork-tender, 10 to 15 minutes.

**2** Uncover and stir in the tomatoes, lime juice, and brown sugar. Cover again and cook for 5 more minutes over low heat—the tomatoes should be softened but still intact, the lime juice still bright. Add more sugar or salt or lime juice as you like. Make sure the *kaddu* doesn't turn to mush; it should maintain some texture. Sprinkle with the cilantro and serve hot.

# ZUNI SPICY BROCCOLI AND CAULIFLOWER

In Judy Rodgers's seminal *Zuni Cafe Cookbook* this is a pasta sauce; in my house it became the de facto way to do a nice job of cooking cruciferous vegetables in a Mediterranean style.

MAKES 4 SERVINGS

| | |
|---|---|
| **1 C** | bread crumbs |
| **¾ C** | olive oil |
| **¾ lb** | broccoli, trimmed, with a few inches of stem intact |
| **¾ lb** | cauliflower, leaves removed and stem end trimmed flush |
| **+** | kosher salt |
| **1 T** | capers, rinsed, pressed dry between towels, and chopped |
| **1 T** | chopped anchovy fillets (optional but nice) |
| **2 T** | chopped garlic |
| **½ t** | fennel seeds, lightly pounded in a mortar |
| **½ t** | chili flakes |
| **2 T** | coarsely chopped flat-leaf parsley |
| **¼ C** | coarsely chopped pitted black olives, such as Niçoise, Gaeta, or Nyons |

**1** Heat the oven to 425°F.

**2** Toss the bread crumbs with 1 tablespoon of the olive oil, spread on a baking sheet, and bake until golden, about 5 minutes. Keep the crumbs on the stovetop until needed.

**3** Cut the broccoli and cauliflower generally lengthwise into slices about ⅛ inch thick. As Ms. Rodgers put it, "Most of the slices will break apart as you produce them, yielding a pile of smooth stem pieces, tiny green broccoli buds, loose cauliflower crumbs, and a few delicate slabs with stem and flower both. Don't worry if the slices are of uneven thickness; that will make for more textural variety."

**4** Warm ¼ cup of the oil in a 12-inch skillet over medium heat. After a couple of minutes, when the oil is hot but not scorching, get to cooking the vegetables in batches: Add enough of the broccoli and cauliflower to fill the pan but not so much that it won't brown. Start with the big pieces; sprinkle them with salt. When they've taken on some color, stir them once and let them color some more; their edges should be crisp in places and burnt in others. Remove them to a plate as they are done. Finish the rest of the vegetables in one or two more batches, adding more oil with each new load of vegetables.

**5** Scrape all the little crumbs of cauliflower and broccoli into the pan with the capers and cook for a few minutes, until the veggie crumbs are crisping and browning. Add the cooked vegetables back to the pan and cook, turning, until combined. Stir in the chopped anchovy (if using), garlic, fennel, and chili flakes. Cook another few minutes, then add the parsley and olives. Taste and season strongly. Toss with the toasted bread crumbs. Serve hot.

# FRAN'S STUFFED ARTICHOKES

I always thought stuffed artichokes were some kind of pointless hassle, that steaming the thistle flowers and serving them chilled with mayonnaise on the side was the only not-insane way to make them at home. But then managing editor Joanna Sciarrino volunteered her mom's special Palm Sunday recipe (thanks, Fran!); consider me a believer. Hallelujah.

**MAKES 4 SERVINGS**

| | |
|---|---|
| **2 C** | Italian-style bread crumbs (plain is okay, but it's always nice when Mr. Progresso sneaks in the MSG for you) |
| **½ C** | grated parmesan cheese |
| **¼ C** | chopped parsley |
| **2 T** | chopped garlic |
| **1 t** | kosher salt |
| **½ t** | freshly ground black pepper |
| **½ C** | extra-virgin olive oil, plus more for drizzling |
| **4** | large artichokes |
| **2 T** | fresh lemon juice |

**1** Combine the bread crumbs, parmesan, parsley, garlic, salt, and pepper in a large bowl. Slowly add the olive oil, stirring as you pour, until the crumb mixture is moistened enough to stick together. Set aside.

**2** Trim the artichoke stems off so the artichokes have level bottoms and sit flat. Trim off the pointed tips of each leaf, then rinse each artichoke thoroughly.

**3** Place the artichokes in a large pot of cold water (one-half to three-quarters full) and add the lemon juice. Bring to a boil over high heat. Reduce the heat and simmer for another 20 minutes. Remove the artichokes and arrange upside down to drain and cool.

**4** Heat the oven to 400°F.

**5** Working with one artichoke at a time, set it in the middle of the bowl of bread crumbs and begin stuffing each leaf with some of the bread-crumb mixture. As you loosen the leaves, take care not to tear them off the artichoke. Brush off any excess crumbs from the outside of the artichoke and place in a large, wide Dutch oven. Repeat with the remaining artichokes, using all the bread crumbs and fitting them snugly together in the pot.

**6** Pour 1 cup of water into the bottom of the pot, then drizzle about 2 tablespoons of olive oil over the tops of the stuffed artichokes. Cover the pot and set over high heat until you can hear the water boiling, then carefully transfer the pot to the oven. Bake, covered, for 10 minutes, then remove the lid and bake until the artichokes are browned and some of the bread crumbs are too, another 20 to 30 minutes. Remove the artichokes from the oven and cool slightly before serving. Artichokes are equally, or possibly more, delicious at room temperature.

# *FOIL-WRAPPED VEGETABLES*

Vegetables get a sorry shake at many barbecues and backyard cookouts. The meat takes precedence and there's only so much space on the grill, so by the time you can put your underseasoned veggie kebabs on you're trying to char veggies over a dying fire.

So what to do? This: Wrap serving sizes of vegetables in foil and set them in coals or set on the edge of the grill while cooking the rest of your meal. They will cook deliciously inside and, for the most part, other than wanting a little salt before you eat them, require little embellishment.

These fall under the EASE IS POWER ruling, but they are also a great advertisement for the galactic completeness of vegetables: With nothing but fire added, they have all the flavor they need inside their skins. Our recommendations for foil-wrapping vegetables are as follows, though you can really trust your inner cowboy on these.

**MAKES AS MUCH AS YOU WANT**

## SWEET POTATOES

Wrap in foil. Cook in the coals for 45 minutes to 1 hour.

## POTATOES

Wrap in foil. Cook in the coals or on the grate, 30 minutes to 1 hour. Maybe dress them like a baked potato when they come off? Just a thought.

## BEETS

Wrap in foil. Cook in the coals, 30 minutes to 1 hour. Use as you would a roasted beet; put them in the refrigerator overnight and toss them in a salad; drizzle with balsamic vinegar.

## GARLIC

Cut off the top of a head of garlic and add oil and salt; wrap in foil, cinching at the top. Set at the edge of the coals for 20 to 30 minutes, turning occasionally so it cooks evenly. Squeeze it out onto bread, which you have also grilled! Now it is garlic bread!

## SQUASH

Go rustico and roast whole in the coals, or, for expedience, cut them into halves or wedges, add a pat of butter or teaspoon of oil, season with salt, wrap in foil, and cook on the grate. Figure 30 minutes and test it with a sharp knife if you're unsure: It should offer little if any resistance.

## CARAMELIZED CABBAGE WITH BUTTER

Lay wedges of cabbage on foil, add a dab of butter, and wrap. Cook on the grate over direct heat for 30 minutes (or more), unwrap, and eat.

# NISHI SWEET POTATO

Nishi is the 327th Momofuku restaurant to open but the first where Joshua Pinsky is the chef. The restaurant opened while we were putting this book together and this side dish was the one dish that really bowled me over the first night I ate there. I love it because it treats the sweet potato like a foodstuff worth actually and actively cooking, which it is. I love it because it hits sweet and hot and sour and umami and salty all pretty hard, and because the combination of flavors isn't immediately obvious but is immediately likable. At Nishi, Pinsky finishes the potato with a shower of crisp microscopic fried Japanese anchovies that are too obscure for me to source, so I absolve you of having to do it either. That said, if you can track down a bottle of *benímosu* (purple sweet potato vinegar) like they use at Momofuku, sub it for the sherry vinegar here. It's delicious and versatile and, unlike the little fish, it lasts forever.

**MAKES 4 SERVINGS**

| | |
|---|---|
| **2 T** | neutral oil |
| **2** | garlic cloves, thinly sliced |
| **¼ C** | hoisin sauce |
| **1 T** | sherry vinegar |
| **1 t** | fish sauce |
| **4** | medium sweet potatoes, preferably ones with purple skin and white flesh |
| **1** | finger, Holland, or Fresno chili, thinly sliced |
| **8** | large mint leaves, cut into ½" squares |

**1** Combine the oil and garlic in a small saucepan and set over medium heat. Heat the oil until the garlic sizzles. Shake the pan as the garlic cooks, caramelizing it evenly. When the garlic is dirty blond, carefully add the hoisin and sherry vinegar and bring to a simmer. Cook for a couple of minutes until the sauce is syrupy. Remove from the heat and stir in the fish sauce. Set the glaze aside.

**2** Heat the oven to 350°F. Line a baking sheet with foil.

**3** Arrange the sweet potatoes on the lined baking sheet and roast them until they are just cooked through, about 40 minutes. A paring knife inserted into one of the potatoes will meet very little resistance. Remove the potatoes from the oven. Leave the oven on and reduce the temperature to 240°F.

**4** Meanwhile, light a fire in your charcoal grill (or turn your propane grill on to medium-high heat if they won't let you cook with live fire in your subdivision). Set the potatoes over the hottest part of the grill. Char the potatoes, turning so they color evenly, until they are blackened on the outside, no more than 10 minutes.

**5** Return the potatoes to the baking sheet and place on the upper rack of the oven. Fill a roasting dish with 1 inch of water and place it on the lower rack. Roast the potatoes with steam until they are extremely tender, the skin is soft, and caramel pours from the ends, another 40 minutes. The potato will have mashed itself inside the skin.

**6** Handling the potatoes gently, slice open a seam along the top. Brush the insides and outs of the potatoes with some of the glaze. Sprinkle with the chili slices and mint squares.

# SARSON KA SAAG

This is one of those dishes that has a ratio of flavor and complexity to effort that's completely out of whack—and the bank error is in your favor. It's a smooth, thick purée of greens, where the pepperiness and bitterness of the mustard greens are in perfect push-and-pull harmony with the spinach, which contributes softness and sweetness. That strongly green flavor is rounded out with butter or ghee and given personality by a tactical strike force of Indian aromatics: few but ruthlessly effective. *Sarson ka saag* is not dependent on sparkling produce from a farmers' market, and it doesn't call for anything hard to find (you could add ¼ teaspoon hing if you have it on hand and that appeals). If all you have is it and some basmati rice, you won't have the worst meal of your life. Pair it with dal (or other legumes) to do it properly, or substitute it for creamed spinach in your life, since it is clearly so much more powerful.

**MAKES 4 SERVINGS**

| | |
|---|---|
| + | kosher salt |
| 1½ lb | mustard greens (from 2 bunches), stemmed and roughly chopped |
| 1 lb | spinach (from 1 large bunch), stemmed, or 1 package (10 oz) frozen spinach, thawed |
| 4 T | ghee or unsalted butter |
| ½ C | minced onion |
| 3 | garlic cloves, grated |
| 1 T | grated fresh ginger |
| 1 | serrano chili, minced |
| ¼ t | garam masala or more to taste (optional) |

**1** Bring a large pot of salted water to a boil. Add the mustard greens, give them a 30-second head start, then add the spinach. Blanch the greens until completely wilted but still bright green, about 3 minutes total. Remove them with a slotted spoon, shake off any excess moisture, and transfer them to a blender. Process until smooth and set aside.

**2** Heat the ghee (or butter) in a large nonstick skillet over medium heat. After a minute, add the onion and cook, stirring occasionally, until softened and starting to go golden, about 8 minutes. Add the garlic and ginger and cook, stirring, until soft and aromatic, about 2 minutes.

**3** Add the chili and the reserved greens purée and stir with a silicone spatula to incorporate the aromatics. Increase the heat to medium and cook, stirring, until a rim of ghee reappears around the edge of the pan, about 10 minutes. Season the mixture with salt (and the garam masala, if you like) and serve hot.

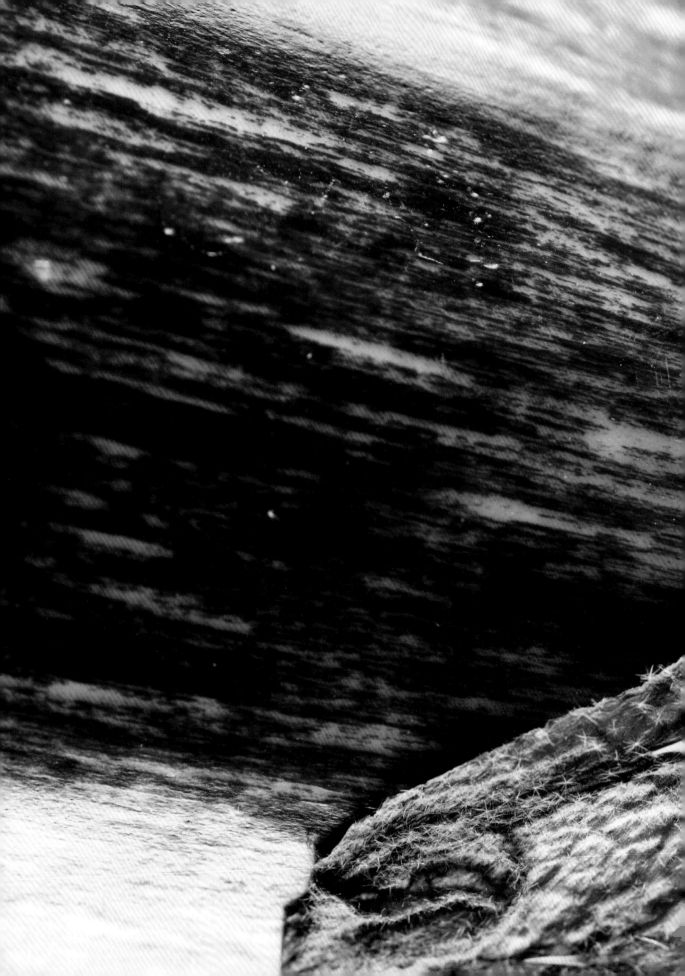

MAINS

# BUTTERNUT SQUASH WITH PIQUILLO CREMA

This is a de-engineered Rick Bayless pasta recipe. Serve it as is and it's a rich vegetable side dish. Toss it with noodles for a delicious pasta dinner. Puree it and it'll be a crazy rich butternut squash soup!

■■ ■■ ■■■ ■

**MAKES 4 SERVINGS**

## PIQUILLO CREMA

| | |
|---|---|
| **4** | garlic cloves, peeled |
| **+** | olive oil |
| **1 C** | Mexican crema, heavy cream, or crème fraîche |
| **½ C** | jarred and drained piquillo peppers or 3 fresh red poblano chilies, charred and skins removed, sliced into strips |
| **1 t** | kosher salt |

## SQUASH

| | |
|---|---|
| **2 lb** | peeled butternut squash |
| **2 T** | reserved garlic oil or olive oil |
| **+** | kosher salt |
| **1 C** | grated Mexican queso añejo, Pecorino Romano, or parmesan |
| **¼ C** | coarsely chopped cilantro |

**1** Make the garlic confit: Put the garlic in a small pot with just enough olive oil to float the cloves. Set over medium heat until bubbles form around the garlic (the oil will be about 185°F). Reduce the heat to low to maintain the temperature and confit the garlic until it is very soft and lightly golden brown, about 20 minutes. Strain the garlic out and reserve the oil.

**2** Warm the crema (or one of its stand-ins) in a glass measuring cup in a microwave for 1 minute at 50 percent power. Pour into the blender with the peppers, garlic, and salt and blend until smooth. Set aside.

**3** Prepare the squash: Heat the oven to 400°F. Cut the peeled squash into cubes and toss with the oil and season with salt. Arrange in an even layer on a sheet pan. Roast, tossing occasionally, until just tender and golden brown, about 30 minutes.

**4** Pour the crema-pepper mixture into a large (10-inch) skillet set over low heat. Add the roasted squash and toss to combine. Stir in ½ cup of the cheese and divide among 4 bowls. Top each bowl with a portion of the remaining cheese and sprinkle with cilantro.

**OR**

Pour the crema-pepper mixture into a large (10-inch) skillet set over low heat. Stir in ½ cup of the cheese until it's warmed through and completely melted. Divide the roasted squash among 4 bowls and top each with crema, a portion of the remaining cheese, and a sprinkle of cilantro.

# MEMELITAS WITH VEGETABLE PEELER SALAD

Let's start at the beginning: Hannah, my wife, started making this for our family after she read in a glossier food magazine than *Lucky Peach* that Alice Waters used to make a snack like this for her daughter. It was never a dish for guests, but it was something we came to rely on and that I actively looked forward to, and it was more vegetably than just quesadillas, which are what the children want to eat most of the time anyway.

Then when we were in Los Angeles, we went to Guelaguetza, an epic and beyond-wonderful Oaxacan restaurant, and what did they have on the kids' menu? Tortillas smeared with beans and covered in melted cheese called *memelitas* (along with French fries and a little bowl of lime-spiked chicken soup; it made me wish I was a kid).

The "vegetable peeler" salad just refers to the "method" of slicing up any firm-fleshed vegetables very thinly using a peeler. You could add fennel, kohlrabi, peppers, broccoli stems, whatever sturdy veg is lurking in the fridge. The 15 or so minutes between making the salad and getting the memelitas on the table gives the lime and salt a chance to break them down a little bit and make them pickley and peppy.

**■ ■ ■**

**MAKES 4 SERVINGS**

## SALAD

|   |   |
|---|---|
| **2** | large carrots, peeled, then shaved with a vegetable peeler |
| **4** | radishes, thinly sliced or shaved (watermelon radishes are nice if you can score 'em!) |
| **1 C** | thinly sliced white cabbage |
| **½ t** | kosher salt |
| **1** | lime, juiced |

## MEMELITAS

|   |   |
|---|---|
| **12** | corn tortillas |
| **1 C** | refried beans (canned are fine) |
| **½ lb** | fresh torn or shredded cheese, preferably Oaxacan, though mozzarella will do and I've used Monterey Jack in a pinch |
| **+** | lime wedges |
| **+** | avocado slices |
| **+** | hot sauce |

**1** Make the "salad": Combine the carrots, radishes, and cabbage in a bowl. Add the salt and lime juice, then toss to coat and set aside while you assemble the *memelitas*.

**2** Make the memelitas: Spread each tortilla with a tablespoon or so of the refried beans and top with the cheese. Warm the memelitas in a toaster oven or regular oven set to broil, until the cheese is melted, 2 to 3 minutes

**3** Top each memelita with a three-finger pinch of salad and serve with lime wedges, sliced avocado, and hot sauce on the side.

# SPANAKORIZO

*Spanakorizo* looks like a humdrum pile of spinach and rice, an Aegean mom's Tuesday-night fallback. But— and I know we're supposed to love all our children equally—it has emerged, at the end of the book-making process, as my favorite dish out of the whole volume.

There's something about the unification of rice and greens that makes this dish feel "complete" and satisfying in a dog-scratching-its-deepest-itch sort of way; something about the way that mess of onions and garlic and leek and dill don't exactly disappear into the dish but don't stand out to be noticed. Spana-korizo is a dish that's greater than the sum of its parts, better than it has any right to be, and certain to be a fixture of my table—and hopefully yours—for years to come.

**MAKES 4 SERVINGS**

½ **C**  olive oil, plus more for finishing

1  onion, cut in half and thinly sliced into half-moons

1  bunch scallions, thinly sliced

1  leek, white part only, cut in half, rinsed well, and thinly sliced

+  kosher salt

1  package (16 oz) frozen spinach

1  bunch dill, chopped

1 **C**  long-grain rice

1½ **C**  water

+  juice of 1½ lemons (cut that extra ½ lemon into wedges and bring to the table)

+  freshly ground black pepper

**1** Heat ¼ cup of the olive oil over medium-high heat in a pot large enough to eventually host the whole party. After a minute, add the onion, scallions, and leek and a large pinch of salt. Sauté the onion mixture, stirring occasionally, until it has wilted, maybe 5 minutes. Stir in the spinach, dill, and another pinch of salt and sauté, stirring until all are wilted, probably fewer but certainly no more than 5 minutes.

**2** Add the rice, water, remaining oil, and lemon juice and bring to a boil. Reduce the heat to low and cover; cook for 15 minutes. Take the pan off the heat and let rest unmolested for 10 minutes before serving. Zazz the spanakorizo up with salt, pepper, additional oil (glug it on like a Greek grandma), and fresh lemon before it goes to the table. Εβιβα!

# MALFATTI IN BROWN BUTTER WITH SAGE

Gnocchi and gnudi became pillowy pastas of prominence in the last decade; potato is the vegetable that powers them both. Malfatti is a member of that same pasta family in that it offers an equally elegant eating experience except it is made with a whole mess of cooked-down and wrung-out greens. Virtue and luxury have never looked so good together.

**MAKES 4 SERVINGS**

| | |
|---|---|
| **12 oz** | fresh ricotta cheese |
| **+** | kosher salt |
| **3 lb** | Swiss chard or lacinato kale, stemmed and roughly chopped |
| **4 T** | unsalted butter, melted, plus 1 stick (4 oz) for serving |
| **¼ C** | fine dried bread crumbs |
| **2** | eggs, beaten |
| **+** | whole nutmeg |
| **+** | freshly ground black pepper |
| **16** | fresh sage leaves |
| **+** | parmesan cheese |

**1** Place the ricotta in a fine-mesh strainer or cheesecloth and let drain overnight in the refrigerator.

**2** Bring a large pot of water to a boil, salt it generously, and blanch the greens until tender but still bright green, 3 to 4 minutes. Drain and squeeze them dry. Place the greens in a clean kitchen towel, gather the corners, and squeeze to extract as much liquid as possible from the greens. Finely chop the greens. Return them to the kitchen towel and squeeze once more. There will be about 1 cup of greens if you've squeezed them well. Unwrap and toss with your fingers to separate the strands.

**3** Combine the drained ricotta, squeezed greens, 4 tablespoons melted butter, the bread crumbs, and eggs in a large bowl. Break up the ricotta with a spoon, then fold in with the other ingredients. Grate some nutmeg over the bowl, season with ½ teaspoon salt and ¼ teaspoon black pepper, and stir the seasonings in.

**4** Scoop or roll the malfatti into 1-ounce egg-shaped dumplings (you will have 20 to 24 dumplings). Lay them like soldiers on a parchment-lined baking sheet. (Malfatti can be frozen like this, if you like. Pop the frozen dumplings from the tray and store in the freezer in a zip-top bag for up to 1 month.)

**5** Bring a large pot of water to a boil and salt it well. Cook the malfatti in batches of 10 to 12, adding them to the pot one by one and distributing them around the pot so they do not stick to one another. They are done when they float to the surface and more than half of each dumpling bobs above the surface of the water, about 8 minutes. Malfatti should be evenly cooked through when done; to test for doneness, cut one in half. The texture of the dumpling should be fluffy and uniform throughout.

**6** While the malfatti are cooking, heat the remaining butter in a wide skillet. Add the sage leaves and a generous pinch of salt. Set the skillet over medium-low heat and allow the butter to gently melt and begin to brown. The sage leaves will sizzle and become golden and crunchy.

**7** When the butter is browned and the sizzling subsides, remove the pan from the heat and add the malfatti. Gently toss the dumplings to coat them in the brown butter, then divide them among pasta bowls. Shower with parmesan and serve hot.

# JESSICA KOSLOW

**SQIRL, LOS ANGELES**

**PM:** What is a power vegetable to you?

**JK:** I think it's two-pronged. A power vegetable can be a meaty vegetable, like Brussels sprouts: They have such a heft and weight that they can take the place of the meat. Broccoli, cauliflower, too. And then there are the things that smash really well: potatoes, squash, parsnips, carrots.

But for me, there's also the power vegetable that can lift you up, the kind that's all about lightness—the lettuces, the celtuce. I'm hoping that you find a way to put sprouts in the book. Things that are nutrient rich and that you're eating raw. They're vibrant. They remind you that the world is alive.

**PM:** I'm more of a burn-your-vegetables-and-soak-them-in-umami kind of guy. What's life like when you look at it through turmeric-juice-colored glasses?

**JK:** Like a shaved Brussels sprout salad with a lot of acid. Or roasted delicata squash, but served cold and finished with pumpkin seed oil and toasted pumpkin seeds, sprouts, pomegranate, and a green sauce and yogurt. We'll serve these things warm too, but in a context where you want more of a salad—more of a live food—we'll serve them cold. That way, you're able to get a certain vibrancy from a vegetable you may look at as something to be burned and seared and charred. You can flip it the other way, and make it feel more alive. And you get that totally other extreme from the kind of power vegetable that you're talking about.

And I don't think you should discount sprouting—not just sprouts as a garnish or finishing touch, which, aside from being a little pricey, are a great and wildly easy way to make a dish prettier and tastier—but sprouting your grains and legumes. We sprout mung beans and all sorts of foods I like to think of as "pods." I think sprouting makes them more delicious, they feel more "alive," and they certainly cook more quickly.

Sprouts have always had a special place in my heart, though—when I was a kid I used to go to the market with my mom, bring home a big bag of sprouts, dump them in a salad bowl with olive oil and lemon and a can of tuna and it was one of my favorite make-it-myself lunches.

**PM:** We both know that vegetables aren't boring, but what are the techniques that you use to make vegetables exciting? You've got roasted squash, it's cold, it's got a number of different condiments on it, it's got sweetness, it's got acid. What's in your bag of tricks to make vegetables more vibrant?

**JK:** I think the sweet and the sour and the salt play. They all play. And on top of that, there's some sort of textural component like toasted buckwheat groats, oven-dehydrated quinoa, or a candied granola. That crunchiness.

I think we all grew up eating bags of chips and Rice Krispies Treats, and we want the crunch. So there's gotta be that textural component. That's a satisfying thing for many people. Once you play those flavors—sweet, salty, savory—and then finish it with something that's maybe not necessarily bread crumbs, you've got them.

Beyond that, though, I think it's important to think about what you're cooking and when and where it's coming from. I don't think that all the people who come to eat at Sqirl are at the farmers' market all the time like we are; they may not know they're eating during the narrow window when we can finish their lentil soup with sprouting broccoli flowers. But we do, and it makes us happy to know we're connecting the people we're feeding to what's happening in the unpaved, beautiful world outside the city. I think there's "power" in that, too!

# ROASTED SQUASH WITH PIPIÁN ROJO

*Pipián rojo* is a member of the greater mole family. (That's *mo-lay,* the delicious category of Mexican sauces, not moles, those disgusting subterranean animals.) It has a complex flavor and an opulent richness that doesn't come from animal fat, like so many European sauces, but from ground pumpkin seeds. (Other pipiáns and moles are thickened with tortillas, or masa, or nuts; it's a fascinating world to explore.)

Pipián rojo would make a pile of junk mail taste good, but since some people might not consider junk mail to be a vegetable, we've paired it here with roasted kabocha squash, which is one of those vegetables that's so good it'd be okay with junk-mail sauce poured over it. But we don't have the recipe for that.

I like to eat this with a big pile of warmed tortillas, though it is self-sufficient enough to work on its own, and perfectly comfortable on top of a bowl of rice or some other hipper grain.

**MAKES 4 SERVINGS**

- **2** 2 lb kabocha squashes
- **+** kosher salt
- **+** Pipián Rojo (page 196)
- **+** sesame seeds
- **+** lime cheeks

**1** Heat the oven to 375°F. Line a baking sheet with parchment paper.

**2** With a sharp, heavy knife, cut the kabochas in half vertically through the stem end. Don't remove the seeds. Lay the halves cut side down on the lined baking sheet. Roast the squashes until they are tender enough to be pierced with a paring knife, 30 to 40 minutes. The skin may be quite firm but the flesh will, at that point, be soft and caramelized in spots.

**3** When the squashes are cool enough to handle, flip them over and carefully scoop out their seeds and pulp, taking care not to break the flesh. Slide a large serving spoon between the skin and flesh of the squash, removing the flesh from each half in two or three large wedges.

**4** Place the wedges from each half into a shallow bowl or dinner plate, season with salt, and blanket each with *pipián rojo*. Sprinkle with sesame seeds and serve with a lime cheek.

# PIPIÁN ROJO

**MAKES 2½ CUPS (4 TO 6 SERVINGS)**

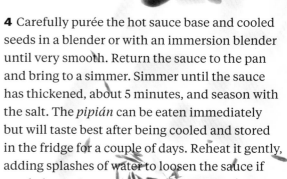

|   |   |
|---|---|
| 3 | dried guajillo chilies |
| 2 | dried ancho chilies (or 2 more guajillos) |
| 2 T | neutral oil |
| 3 | garlic cloves |
| ½ C | chopped onion |
| 2 | bay leaves |
| 1 t | dried oregano |
| ½ t | ground cumin |
| ½ t | sweet paprika |
| ⅛ t | ground cinnamon |
| 4 C | water |
| ½ C | pumpkin seeds |
| 2 T | sesame seeds |
| 1 t | kosher salt |

**1** Pull the stems from the chilies and shake out and discard their seeds. Tear the chilies into pieces the size of a postage stamp.

**2** Heat the oil in a large, heavy skillet over medium-low heat. Add the torn chilies, garlic, and onion, and toss to coat them in the oil. Sweat the vegetables until the onion and garlic are soft and the oil has turned red from the chilies, about 8 minutes. Stir in the bay leaves, oregano, cumin, paprika, and cinnamon. Continue cooking, stirring often, until the spices have melded and give off a heady aroma, about 2 minutes. Add the water and bring to a boil. Reduce the heat and gently simmer until the sauce base has reduced by half (to about 2 cups), about 20 minutes.

**3** Meanwhile, place the pumpkin seeds in a medium skillet and set over medium-low heat. Warm the seeds, tossing them in the pan so that they toast evenly, until they have darkened a few shades, 3 to 4 minutes. A few will pop and dance in the pan. Slide them onto a plate and add the sesame seeds to the pan. Toast the seeds, shaking the pan, until they are a dirty blond, about 2 minutes. Slide them onto the plate with the pumpkin seeds and let cool.

**4** Carefully purée the hot sauce base and cooled seeds in a blender or with an immersion blender until very smooth. Return the sauce to the pan and bring to a simmer. Simmer until the sauce has thickened, about 5 minutes, and season with the salt. The *pipián* can be eaten immediately but will taste best after being cooled and stored in the fridge for a couple of days. Reheat it gently, adding splashes of water to loosen the sauce if needed.

# SWEET POTATO BURRITOS

In this evening's production of YOUR BURRITO, the role of Chorizo will be played by its understudy, Sweet Potato. Please remember to silence your cell phones before the show begins.

**MAKES 4 SERVINGS**

| | |
|---|---|
| **1½ lb** | sweet potatoes, peeled and cut into ½" pieces |
| **1 T** | neutral oil |
| **1 t** | kosher salt |
| **¼ t** | freshly ground black pepper |
| **2 t** | chili powder |
| **¼ t** | ground cumin |
| **¼ t** | ground coriander |
| **½ t** | oregano |
| **+** | pinch ground cinnamon |
| **+** | pinch ground cloves |
| **4** | 12" flour tortillas |

## TO PUT IN YOUR BURRITO

- cooked rice
- cooked beans
- Salsa Verde (page 202)
- avocado slices
- Pico de Gallo (page 66)
- sour cream
- shredded cheese
- cilantro leaves
- thinly sliced iceberg lettuce
- pickled jalapeño chilies

**1** Heat the oven to 400°F. Line a baking sheet with parchment paper.

**2** Combine the sweet potatoes, oil, salt, cumin, chili powder, coriander, and black pepper in a bowl and toss to coat. Arrange in a single layer on the lined baking sheet and roast until tender and caramelized, about 30 minutes.

**3** Assemble the burritos. See the following pages for burrito-filling instructions.

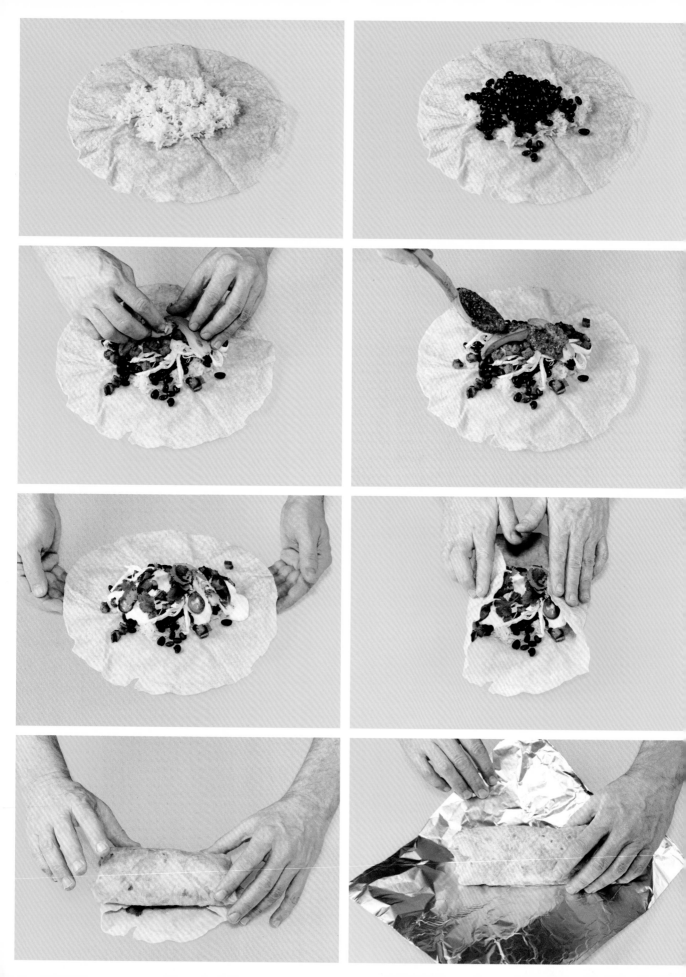

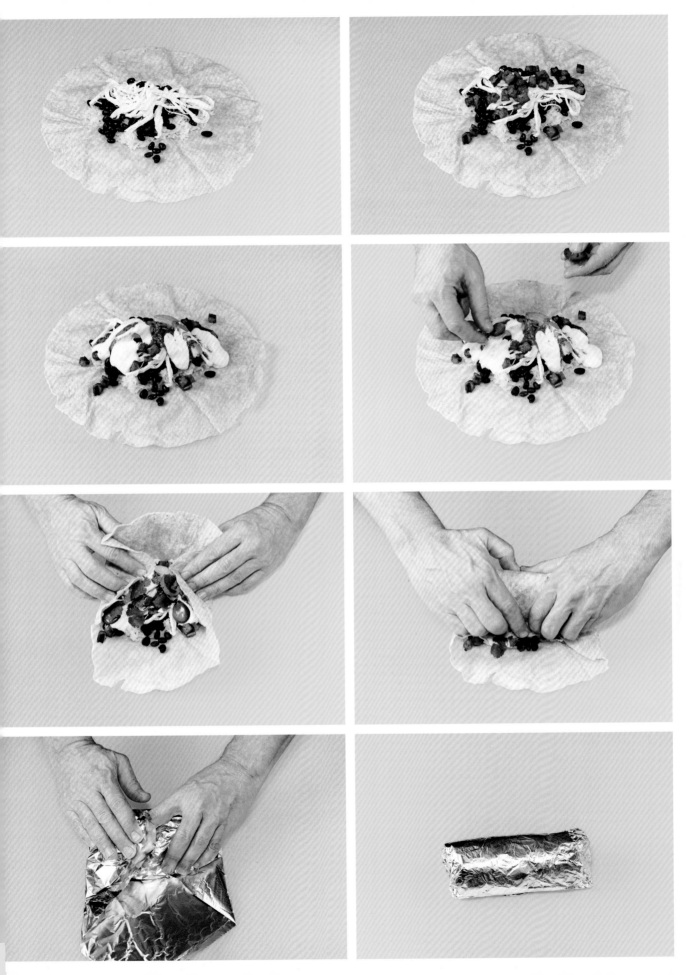

# SALSA VERDE

I learned to make salsa verde this way from Marc Meyer, the first chef I ever worked on a cookbook with. I like it more than any other salsa verde except the one at La Super Rica taqueria in Santa Barbara, California, but I can't for the life of me figure out how they do it. For us mortals, this will do.

**MAKES 3 CUPS**

| | |
|---|---|
| **1 lb** | tomatillos |
| **1** | medium onion, cut into ½"-thick rings |
| **8** | garlic cloves, unpeeled |
| **1** | jalapeño chili |
| **+** | neutral oil |
| **¼ C** | chopped cilantro stems + ¼ C cilantro leaves |
| **1 t** | kosher salt |
| **+** | fresh lime juice |

**1** Heat the broiler to high.

**2** Dunk the tomatillos in a bowl of hot water to dissolve the sticky sap on their skin and loosen their papery sheaths. Remove and discard the papery outsides. Rub the tomatillos, onion slices, garlic cloves, and jalapeño with oil to coat and arrange them on a rimmed baking sheet. Broil the vegetables, turning once, until they are charred (actually charred, not just browned) and softened, about 10 minutes. Remove from the broiler and cool them enough to handle.

**3** Trim the stem from the jalapeño (and scrape out the seeds, if you want less heat), squeeze the garlic cloves out of their skins, and transfer them and the tomatillos and onion to a blender or food processor and process until smooth. Add the cilantro and salt and continue processing until very smooth. Taste the salsa and adjust the seasoning with a pinch of salt or squeeze of lime juice as needed.

# SALTIE'S CLEAN SLATE

The sandwich is a coalition of the willing: a coalition of elements that are all willing to be AWESOME. The hummus has MISO in it. The pickled beets are ROASTED. The naan is truly, honestly easy to make and criminally good. You can add other herbs (dill!) or other pickled things (they often have turmeric-yellow bread-and-butter-style pickled onions) on there too, but don't skip out on any of the following. If your commitment to *Power!* and/or awesomeness is weak, at least try making the naan before you write off this recipe as too complicated—it'll draw you into trying the rest!

For those wondering where such a wonderful sandwich comes from: Her creator is Caroline Fidanza, a chef who, during her decade at Diner, did the most honest market-driven cooking in the city at a time when everybody else was pretending at it, and helped to codify the idea of a Brooklyn restaurant—the idea that's been exported and repackaged around the world since. You can score her handiwork these days at Saltie, a tiny slip of a spot on Metropolitan Avenue in Williamsburg, Brooklyn.

▬▬ ▬ ▬ ▬

**MAKES 4 SANDWICHES**

## YOGURT SAUCE

| | |
|---|---|
| ½ C | plain whole-milk yogurt |
| 1 T | olive oil |
| 1 t | white wine vinegar |
| ½ t | ground sumac |
| + | kosher salt |

## SANDWICHES

| | |
|---|---|
| 4 | pieces cooked Naan (page 210) |
| 1 C | Hummus (page 42) |
| 1 C | cooked quinoa |
| 1 C | bite-size pieces of Pickled Beets (page 208) |
| ½ C | julienned carrots |
| ½ C | julienned radishes |
| ¼ C | torn fresh mint |
| ¼ C | sliced scallions |

**1** Make the yogurt sauce: Stir the yogurt, olive oil, vinegar, and sumac together in a small bowl. Season lightly with salt. Refrigerate until ready to use.

**2** Assemble the sandwiches: Lay one round of naan on a work surface and spread it with ¼ cup hummus. Spread 2 tablespoons of yogurt sauce over the hummus, then sprinkle with ¼ cup quinoa. Arrange the beets, carrots, and radishes on top, then sprinkle with the mint and scallions. Repeat to make 4 sandwiches.

# PICKLED BEETS

**MAKES A QUART CONTAINER'S WORTH**

| | |
|---|---|
| **1 lb** | beets |
| **2 C** | water |
| **1 T** | olive oil |
| **1½ t** | kosher salt |
| **1 C** | red wine vinegar |
| **½ C** | sugar |
| **1 t** | black peppercorns |
| **1 t** | coriander seeds |
| **1 t** | mustard seeds |
| **1** | star anise |
| **3** | allspice berries |

**1** Heat the oven to 400°F.

**2** Fit the beets snugly in a roasting pan and carefully add 1 cup of water. Drizzle with the olive oil and season with 1 teaspoon of the salt. Cover the pan with foil and roast until the beets are tender, about 1 hour. When cool enough to handle, rub the skins from the beets with paper towels and slice into ¼-inch-thick rounds. Place the slices in a jar or bowl.

**3** Combine the red wine vinegar, remaining 1 cup water, sugar, peppercorns, coriander, mustard seeds, star anise, allspice berries, and remaining ½ teaspoon salt in a saucepan. Place over high heat and bring to a simmer, stirring to dissolve the sugar. Pour the hot pickling liquid over the beets, and let cool. Cover and refrigerate for at least 24 hours. Refrigerated, pickles will stay fresh for up to 2 months.

# *NAAN*

**MAKES 4 ROUNDS**

| | |
|---|---|
| **1 C** | all-purpose flour, plus more for dusting |
| **⅓ C** | whole-grain spelt flour or whole wheat flour |
| **½ t** | kosher salt |
| **¼ t** | baking powder |
| **⅔ C** | buttermilk or yogurt |
| **+** | olive oil, for cooking the naan |

**1** Whisk together the flours, salt, and baking powder in a large bowl. Add the buttermilk and stir with a wooden spoon until the dough becomes too stiff to mix. Dust your hands with all-purpose flour and knead the dough in the bowl to form a uniform texture. Shape into a ball, wrap in plastic, and refrigerate for at least 1 hour and up to 1 day.

**2** When ready to make the naan, unwrap the dough, place it on a floured work surface, and divide it into four equal pieces. Dust the pieces with flour and roll them out to 7- to 8-inch rounds.

**3** Heat a cast iron pan over medium-high heat until a wisp of smoke rises from the surface. Drizzle a teaspoon of olive oil into the pan, pick up one piece of dough, pass it between your two hands to shake off excess flour, and lay it in the skillet. Cook the dough until the surface is covered in bubbles, then drizzle with another teaspoon of oil and flip. Continue cooking until the naan is puffy and browned, around 1 minute longer. Remove from the pan and keep warm. Repeat for the remaining pieces of dough.

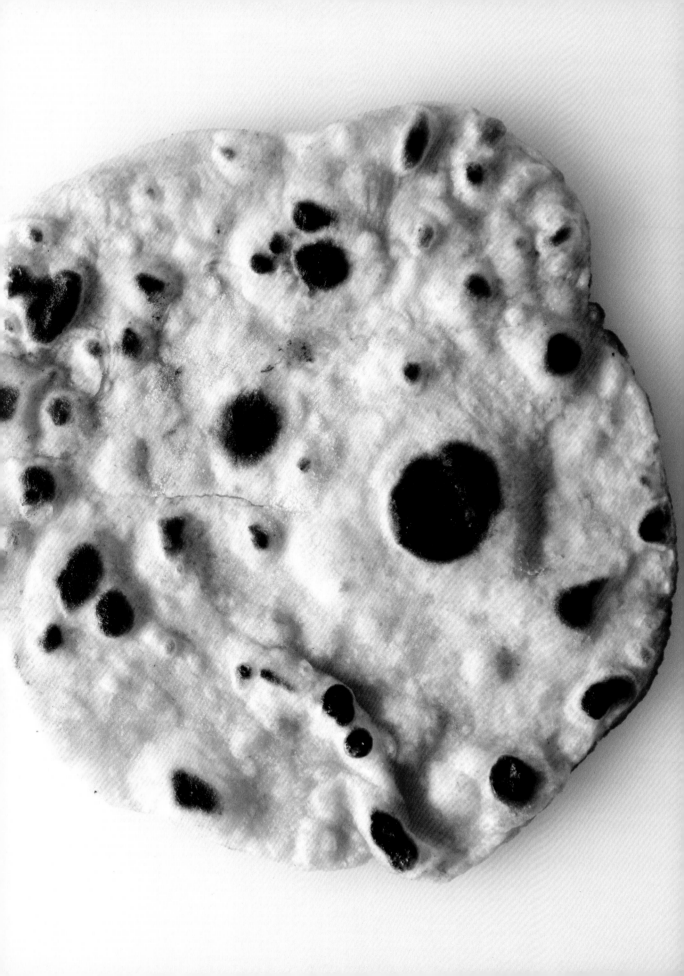

# ROASTED CABBAGE WITH BANANA BLOSSOM DRESSING

Ever wonder why cans of Thai curry paste are so small? Because there's so much POWER in each one. I think of them as little tins of saved time, and use part of one to make the fiery, fragrant dressing for this satisfying and meaty wedge of roasted cabbage. It's a Thai-influenced dish that could happily serve as a main course alongside some sticky or jasmine rice.

The name, should you be wondering, is a tip of the hat to Uncle Boon's, a Thai restaurant in Manhattan—this is a simplified version of the salad dressing they put on finely sliced banana blossoms and, less exotically, charcoal-roasted cabbage.

**MAKES 6 SERVINGS**

- **+** neutral oil
- **1** green or white cabbage (3 lb), cut through the core end into 6 wedges
- **+** kosher salt
- **½ C** coconut milk
- **¼ C** red curry paste
- **3 T** fresh lime juice
- **2 T** fish sauce
- **1 T** sugar
- **+** stuff to scatter on top of the cabbage: peanuts, cilantro leaves, sliced fresh chilies, and/or fried shallots (either homemade—as in steps 1 and 2 of Zucchini Mujadara, page 218—or purchased from a well-stocked Asian supermarket, or use French's fried onions from the supermarket)

**1** Heat the oven to 400°F. Slick a rimmed baking sheet with oil.

**2** Grease up your cabbage wedges: They don't need to shine like hardbodies on Venice Beach, but the oil will help bring the heat to the cabbage, will turn it tender inside and crisp outside, and that's how you want it to be. Sprinkle your cabbies with salt and pop the tray of 'em into the oven. They will take about 40 minutes to cook through, and you'll want to flip them once midway on their journey, to ensure even browning. You know they're ready when the core end offers no meaningful resistance to the tip of a sharp knife.

**3** While the cabbage is cooking, make the dressing: Combine 1 tablespoon of oil, the coconut milk, curry paste, lime juice, fish sauce, and sugar in a blender or a container into which you can insert an immersion blender or a jar with a lid that you can shake the bejesus out of it. Regardless of the method, you're looking to end up with a homogenous, unified dressing. It will keep in the fridge for days should you decide to make it in advance.

**4** The wedges go on plates; the dressing is generously drizzled on top of them. Scatter with garnishes and serve, warm or at room temperature, with a fork and a steak knife, to help cut up the cabbage.

# TOFU AKURI

This is one of my family's recipes, from Coomi Mishra, my brother-in-law's wife's mother. It's usually made with eggs but she substitutes tofu—which makes this a vegan scramble—the sort of thing your cousin who's a freshman at Reed College probably lives off of, except this one is more delicious. Coomi told us, "For us Parsis, it is usually served as a breakfast item. We usually serve it with white sliced bread or with roti or chapati. My memories are also of taking it in the form of a sandwich for school lunches or for a particularly delicious picnic meal." From Coomi's kitchen to yours, for picnics, Parsi and otherwise.

**MAKES 4 SERVINGS**

| | |
|---|---|
| **1** | container extra-firm tofu |
| **2 T** | olive oil |
| **1 C** | finely diced onion |
| **1½ C** | finely diced potato |
| **2 t** | minced garlic |
| **1** | slice (¼") fresh ginger, minced |
| **⅓ C** | water |
| **+** | kosher salt |
| **½ C** | cilantro leaves |
| **1** | plum tomato, seeded and diced |
| **1** | green chili (optional), minced |
| **¼ t** | ground turmeric |
| **+** | freshly ground black pepper |

**1** Drain the tofu and set on a plate lined with several layers of paper towels. Top with another plate and press in this fashion for at least 20 minutes or as long as overnight (in the refrigerator). This will firm the tofu and yield a light and fluffy scramble instead of a soggy one.

**2** Pat the tofu dry. Mash the tofu with a fork, creating small curds resembling scrambled eggs.

**3** Heat the olive oil in a large cast iron skillet over medium-high heat. Add the onion and cook until its edges are translucent and golden, about 5 minutes. Add the potato, garlic, and ginger and cook, stirring often, until the potato picks up some color, about 3 minutes. Add the water and a pinch of salt, cover, reduce the heat to medium-low, and steam the potatoes until they are just tender but not at all falling apart, about 10 minutes.

**4** Uncover and allow any remaining water to steam off before stirring in half of the cilantro (save the rest to garnish the dish), along with the tomato, chili (if using), and turmeric. Cook until the tomato has softened and the bottom of the pan is dry, about 5 minutes.

**5** Fold the tofu into the potato mixture and continue folding until the tofu is heated through, about 3 minutes. Finish with the remaining cilantro and a few grinds of black pepper.

# FALAFEL

The power of falafel is, to me, unquestionable. But the method of making them? I didn't even know there was a debate. Fortunately there is Mary-Frances Heck in my life and in the development and testing of this book she was adamant: We have to use a meat grinder to make our falafel.

Really? I asked sheepishly. A meat grinder in a vegetable book? (I am, of course, a fan of the perverse, particularly the variety of mundane perversity that including a meat grinder counts as, but I dislike summoning outré equipment for its own sake.) She persisted. Most real falafel makers use a grinder, she told me. She told me of side-by-side food processor vs. meat grinder taste tests conducted in kitchens she'd cooked in. She sent me YouTube videos from the Holy Land to demonstrate that this wasn't an academic point being argued by Irish-Americans, but a timeworn truth of the falafel elite. And so I yielded. (She can't stop me from parenthetically noting that you can, of course, use a food processor, but Ms. Heck will say you will be missing out on the uniform little bits of chickpea that fry up crunchy-on-the-outside and fluffy-on-the-inside; that the end product will taste but not feel like falafel.)

Regardless of how you grind your chickpeas, falafel don't fly solo: Pair them with Hummus (page 42), Arab or Israeli Salad (page 68), Tabbouleh (page 72), Laban Khiyar (page 56; not that they'd be bad with any of those yogurt sauces), tahini sauce, Pickled Beets (page 208), and pita or the Naan on page 210.

---

**MAKES 32 PIECES**

| | |
|---|---|
| **1 lb** | dried chickpeas |
| **2** | garlic cloves, chopped |
| **1 C** | chopped onion |
| **1 C** | finely chopped parsley |
| **1 T** | coriander seeds |
| **2 t** | kosher salt |
| **1 t** | ground cumin |
| **½ t** | freshly ground black pepper |
| **+** | peanut or canola oil, for frying |

**1** Place the chickpeas in a large bowl and add water to cover by at least 2 inches. Cover and refrigerate overnight.

**2** Drain the chickpeas and dry out the bowl. Return the chickpeas to the bowl and toss them with the garlic, onion, parsley, coriander, salt, cumin, and pepper.

**3** Assemble a meat grinder with the fine (⅛-inch) die. Pass the chickpea mixture through the grinder twice, taking care not to compact the mixture after it has been ground the second time. (Note, please, that this falafel mix can be bulk-frozen flat in a zip-top bag, or shaped into balls and deposited on a parchment-lined baking sheet, frozen, then transferred to a zip-top bag and stored in the freezer for 1 month.)

**4** Pour 2 inches of oil into a large, heavy pot. Bring the oil to 350°F.

**5** Using a 1-ounce ice cream scoop, shape the falafel mixture into 1-inch balls. (Alternatively, shape 2 tablespoons of the mixture into a ball or hockey puck with your hands, taking care not to pack the mixture too tightly.) Fry them in batches, bobbing and turning them with a spider, until deeply browned, crunchy, and cooked through, about 4 minutes. Drain on paper towels and serve hot.

# ZUCCHINI MUJADARA

I remember the first time my wife, Hannah, made *mujadara* for dinner—I think it was out of Mina Stone's excellent cookbook *Cooking for Artists*. I was pretty down on the idea—how exciting can lentils and rice be, I idiotically thought to myself—and then more or less elbowed my children away from the dinner table as I ate most of the family-size portion. In our version, we use caramelized zucchini in place of the more standard onions, and fried shallots contribute their crunch as a garnish. This is a complete-meal vegetable dish as rewarding as anything with meat in it.

■ ■ ■ ■

**MAKES 6 SERVINGS**

| | |
|---|---|
| ½ **lb** | shallots, peeled |
| 1½ **C** | neutral oil, for frying |
| **+** | kosher salt and freshly ground black pepper |
| 1 **C** | brown lentils, picked over for stones |
| **+** | olive oil |
| 2 | bay leaves |
| 1 **C** | basmati rice, rinsed in cold water until it runs clear |
| 2 **lb** | zucchini, coarsely grated (3 large zucchini) |

**1** Thinly slice the shallots into rings on a mandoline. You can also use a knife, but make the slices as thin and even as possible. There will be about 2 cups of sliced shallots when all is said and done.

**2** Combine the shallots and neutral oil in a wide, high-sided pan suitable for frying. Set the pan over low heat, and let it ride, swirling or stirring occasionally. Avoid the temptation to increase the heat—these shallots will become crisp, not greasy, so be patient. When the shallots are golden brown, after 20 to 30 minutes, remove them from the oil with a strainer to a baking sheet lined with paper towels. Season them with salt and pepper and let them cool. Reserve the cooled shallot oil for cooking zucchini (any extra is lovely in a salad dressing). The fried shallots will stay fresh in an airtight container for a few days.

**3** Cover the lentils with 2 inches of cool water in a medium pot and season with 1 teaspoon of salt. Bring to a simmer, then reduce the heat to medium-low and simmer until just tender, 20 to 25 minutes. Drain the lentils and toss them with 1 tablespoon of olive oil.

**4** While the lentils are cooking, place another medium pot over high heat and add 1½ cups of cold water, the bay leaves, a pinch of salt, and the rice. Bring to a boil, then cover, reduce the heat to low, and cook until all of the water is absorbed, 15 minutes. Remove from the heat and let rest 10 minutes. Fluff the rice with a fork and set aside.

**5** In a skillet, heat ½ cup of the shallot oil over medium-high heat. Squeeze a handful of the grated zucchini, letting the juices drain back in the bowl, and add it to the oil, scattering it around the pan. Fry the zucchini, shaking the pan so the individual strands of zucchini float. When they are light golden and have shrunk to half their size, strain from the oil with a spider or slotted spoon and place on a large plate in a single layer. Repeat with the remaining zucchini, adding olive oil as needed to the pan, until all of it is caramelized.

**6** Toss the lentils and rice together in a large bowl, then fold in the zucchini. Handle the *mujadara* gently, maintaining the individuality of the components and not mashing them together. Dress with a touch more oil or salt if needed, then arrange on a platter. Top with the fried shallots and serve.

# EGGPLANT MARINARA

I wrote a cookbook with the guys from Frankies Spuntino a few years back. It is filled with easy to achieve recipes for their lightened-up take on Italian-American cuisine. They've decided to revise the eggplant recipe in future editions to reflect the way they make it now—more classically, with battered-and-fried nightshades. But I remain steadfastly dedicated to this fairly healthy bastardization of the dish. I am including it here to memorialize its excellence. I will eat this hot or cold, in a sandwich, as a main course, anything. I would eat it in a car, at a bar, with a bear, I would eat it anywhere.

**MAKES 4 TO 6 SERVINGS**

**3** large eggplants, sliced crosswise into ½"-thick disks

**¼ C** olive oil

**+** kosher salt and white pepper

**3 C** tomato sauce (use your own, your grandma's, or the Simple Tomato Sauce on page 34)

**3 C** grated Parmigiano-Reggiano cheese

**½** large ball fresh mozzarella (about 8 oz), cut into ¼"-thick slices (or, if you're feeling fancy, 1 ball of mozzarella di bufala, sliced the same way)

**1** Heat the oven to 350°F.

**2** Toss the sliced eggplant with the olive oil, salt, and white pepper in a large bowl, making sure that the eggplant is evenly dressed. Arrange the eggplant slices in a single layer across two baking sheets. Pop it into the oven for 30 minutes, flipping it once midway, until it's mottled in parts and deeply browned in others and beginning to shrink away from the skin. (You want the eggplant to be pretty delicious looking at this stage; if it looks parcooked, keep it going. You can't really overcook it for these purposes.)

**3** Coat the bottom of a casserole (or other ovenproof vessel appropriate for a lasagna-type preparation) in a thick layer of tomato sauce. Nestle a single layer of eggplant slices into the sauce, sprinkle with salt and pepper, and give the eggplants a good coating of Parmigiano. Repeat the layering—tomato, eggplant, salt and pepper, Parmigiano—until all the ingredients are used, finishing with a layer of Parmigiano. Cover the pan with foil and bake for 1 hour. Serve hot, cold, or in between.

**4** Serve it with a layer of cold mozzarella slices on top of or alongside portions of eggplant.

# MUSHROOMS EN PAPILLOTE (SORT OF)

This is a perfect power vegetable as long as you accept mushrooms as vegetables and, if you don't, we're really too far gone to debate that point now. EASE IS POWER and this is on the embarrassing end of the ease spectrum. It's got tableside panache, it harnesses the fermented umami of soy sauce and the fattiness of butter, and it could make a bowl of rice into dinner (maybe do one of these per person in that case). Or you could serve it with fish or chicken or some other vegetables that will be jealous at its effortless swagger.

**MAKES 1 OR 2 SERVINGS**

| | |
|---|---|
| **½ lb** | mixed mushrooms, trimmed and cut into bite-size pieces |
| **2 T** | unsalted butter |
| **1 T** | soy sauce |
| **+** | freshly ground black pepper |
| **+** | lemon wedges |

**1** Heat the oven to 450°F.

**2** Take a 12-inch square of parchment or foil, fold it in half, then unfold it and pile the mushrooms on one half. Cut the butter into 6 to 8 pieces and arrange over the mushrooms. Drizzle with the soy sauce. Fold the paper or foil over the mushrooms and crimp the open ends to seal the package.

**3** Place the packet on a rimmed baking sheet and roast until the mushrooms are tender, about 20 minutes. Carefully open the packet—the steam will be hot!—preferably at the table. Season with a couple of grinds of pepper and a squeeze of lemon.

# ROOT VEGETABLE TAGINE WITH RED CHERMOULA AND COUSCOUS

As a meat eater (sorry everybody!), my yardstick for our tagine progress was measured in missing links of merguez. This version—which marshals a turbocharged chermoula and works with the sort of underwhelming root cellar–y veggies you can find just about anywhere—passes muster. The chickpeas add body; the raisins add the sweetness it needs. If you have a veggie soirée on the books, this'll do just fine with a nice, chilled Algerian wine.

**MAKES 6 SERVINGS**

## TAGINE

| | |
|---|---|
| **2** | large carrots |
| **1** | bunch baby turnips or 2 medium turnips |
| **2** | waxy, yellow-fleshed potatoes |
| **1** | large sweet potato |
| **1** | small celery root |
| **½ lb** | cipollini onions, peeled |
| **½ C** | cooked (or—who we kidding?—canned) chickpeas |
| **¼ C** | raisins |
| **+** | Red Chermoula (page 226) |

## COUSCOUS

| | |
|---|---|
| **1 C** | dry couscous |
| **1** | cinnamon stick (1") or 1 pinch ground cinnamon |
| **1** | bay leaf |
| **+** | kosher salt |
| **1 T** | unsalted butter |
| **1 C** | boiling water |

**1** Make the tagine: Heat the oven to 325°F. Peel, trim, and chop the carrots, turnips, potatoes, sweet potato, and celery root into approximate 1-inch pieces. Some variation in size is welcome.

**2** Lay down a bed of the onions in a large tagine or Dutch oven. Follow them with the largest chunks of the hardiest vegetables, which you will arrange around the perimeter of the pan. Pile up the chickpeas and raisins in the middle. Scatter the smaller pieces of vegetables over the top. Pour the chermoula over all. If you are using a Dutch oven instead of a sanctioned tagine, tear off an 18-inch sheet of foil. Shape it into a cone with the same diameter as the pot. Place this hat atop the vegetables to mimic the shape of a tagine top, then cover the pan with the lid. It facilitates self-basting, which is kind of the point of tagine cooking.

**3** Slide the tagine into the oven and bake for 1 hour without disturbing it. Remove from the oven and gently toss to combine the ingredients.

**4** Make the couscous: Combine the couscous, cinnamon, bay leaf, salt, and butter in a heatproof bowl. Pour the boiling water over the couscous and cover the bowl with plastic wrap. Let stand for 5 minutes. Uncover and fluff the couscous with a fork.

**5** To serve, dole out portions of the tagine over steaming bowls of couscous, and bring the remainder to the table for your guests to help themselves.

# RED CHERMOULA

**MAKES 2 CUPS**

| | |
|---|---|
| **2 T** | tomato paste |
| **+** | pinch of saffron threads |
| **2 T** | boiling water |
| **2 T** | sweet paprika |
| **1 T** | kosher salt |
| **2 t** | smoked paprika (pimentón) |
| **2 t** | ground cumin |
| **¼ t** | freshly ground black pepper |
| **+** | pinch of cayenne pepper |
| **¾ C** | cool water |
| **¼ C** | chopped parsley |
| **¼ C** | chopped cilantro |
| **2 T** | chopped preserved lemon |
| **2 T** | chopped garlic |
| **2 T** | fresh lemon juice |
| **½ C** | olive oil |

Combine the tomato paste and saffron in a heatproof bowl and add the boiling water, stirring to loosen the tomato paste. Whisk in the sweet paprika, salt, smoked paprika, cumin, black pepper, and cayenne until smooth. Stir in the cool water, then mix in the parsley, cilantro, preserved lemon, garlic, and lemon juice. Finally whisk in the olive oil. Taste for salt and season as needed: It should be a powerful, assertive sauce, something that can burrow to the bland heart of a steamed turnip and make it taste good. Refrigerate until ready to use. It will certainly keep in the fridge for a few days.

# CAULIFLOWER CHAAT

This not-actually-very-Indian-at-all dish celebrates the delicious versatility of cauliflower and the compelling flavor of chaat masala, which marshals *amchoor,* or dried mango powder, to give it the sort of power that the chef Mario Batali would probably celebrate with a #yumbang on the internets. It is not a traditional chaat but a lovingly conceived bastard child of many Indian dishes we dig. I'd happily eat it out of a paper cone or a bowl of rice. The list of optional add-ins is long, but the more of them you can scrape together, the merrier you will be.

**MAKES 4 SERVINGS**

| | |
|---|---|
| **1** | head cauliflower, cut into small florets, stem chopped |
| **1 t** | garam masala |
| **¼ t** | cayenne pepper |
| **1 t** | ground coriander |
| **¼ t** | ground turmeric |
| **¾ t** | fennel seeds |
| **¾ t** | cumin seeds |
| **1 C** | cooked (or canned) chickpeas |
| **2 T** | olive oil |
| **1 t** | kosher salt |
| **+** | freshly ground black pepper |
| **1 t** | chaat masala or amchoor or juice of ½ lemon or lime |
| **¼ C** | chopped cilantro, plus more leaves for garnish |
| **¼ C** | minced red onion |
| **¼ C** | finely chopped tomato |
| **¼ C** | finely chopped cucumber |
| **½ C** | thin yogurt or Raita (page 56) |
| **2–4 T** | maple syrup, sweet tamarind sauce, or chutney |
| **+** | green chutney |
| **1–2** | finely sliced bird's-eye chilies |
| **+** | your favorite hot sauce |

**1** In a large bowl, toss the cauliflower with the garam masala, cayenne, coriander, turmeric, fennel seeds, and cumin seeds until coated. Add the chickpeas, olive oil, salt, and black pepper and toss to combine.

**2** Heat the oven to 450°F. Spread the cauliflower mixture evenly on a sheet pan and roast for 15 minutes, or until everything is looking nice and toasty.

**3** When slightly cooled, toss the mixture with the chaat masala (or amchoor if you have it), chopped cilantro, red onion, tomato, and cucumber.

**4** If you're serving it family-style, garnish with the yogurt, maple syrup, green chutney, cilantro leaves, chilies, and hot sauce. If you're serving it individually, divide into bowls and garnish each separately. Make 'em look nice!

# TOFU CONEY ISLAND

This is a chili dog crossed with cheese fries that does not include cheese, dog, traditional chili, or anything else your average vegan would object to. It is also more satisfying than the typical caveman-on-the-boardwalk type of concoction that its name pays homage to. I can't not greedily power through a plate of it when I'm at Ivan Ramen, and then I am so fat and happy it is hard to slurp down a bowl of his ramen with the appropriate gusto. You will not be similarly challenged when making it at home.

**MAKES 4 SERVINGS**

| | |
|---|---|
| **16 oz** | firm or extra-firm tofu |
| **¼ C** | cornstarch |
| **+** | canola oil, for frying |
| **+** | Miso Mushroom Chili (recipe follows) |
| **4 T** | finely diced yellow onion |
| **+** | yellow mustard |

**1** Cut the tofu into approximately 3 × ½ × ½-inch fries. For added texture, intrigue, and Coney Island authenticity, use a crinkle cutter to shape your fries.

**2** Put the cornstarch in a shallow baking pan and roll the fries around in it to coat them, then shake off the excess.

**3** Pour ¼ inch of oil into a large, high-sided skillet set over medium-high heat. When the oil shimmers, add a handful of tofu fries to the skillet. The oil should come a little more than halfway up the sides of the fries. Cook them until golden and crisp on the first side, about 4 minutes. Turn and cook until crisp on all sides, another 3 to 4 minutes in all. Drain on paper towels. Repeat, adding oil to the pan as needed, until all the fries are fried.

**4** Arrange a pile of fries on each of 4 plates. Smother with a ladleful of hot chili and sprinkle with 1 tablespoon diced onions. Squiggle mustard over the pile.

## MISO MUSHROOM CHILI

This makes more than you need for the tofu fries, but it is a deeply delicious vegetarian chili and I know that you will find another purpose for it.

**MAKES 1 QUART**

| | |
|---|---|
| **¼ C** | canola oil |
| **1** | large onion, diced |
| **1 lb** | button mushrooms |
| **1 t** | kosher salt |
| **1 T** | grated garlic |
| **1 T** | grated fresh ginger |
| **⅔ C** | ketchup |
| **¼ C** | sake |
| **¼ C** | mirin |
| **⅓ C** | red miso |
| **3 T** | soy sauce |
| **3 T** | white vinegar |
| **1 T** | sugar |
| **6–8 oz** | beech or other small tender mushrooms, trimmed and chopped |
| **1 T** | fresh lemon juice |

**1** Heat the oil in a medium pan over low heat. Add the onion, button mushrooms, and salt and cook until the mushrooms release their liquid and the liquid evaporates, about 25 minutes.

**2** Add the garlic and ginger and cook gently for 10 more minutes. Stir in the ketchup, sake, mirin, miso, soy sauce, vinegar, and sugar. Simmer, partially covered, for 15 minutes.

**3** Add the beech mushrooms and lemon juice and cook until the mushrooms have softened, about 5 minutes. Cool or use immediately.

# KUNG PAO CELERIES

This was one of those quixotic missions: What can we do that tastes like junky—but not too junky!— take-out? But takeout that's vegetable-centric? We chose kung pao as our flavor profile, that slightly spicy mix of chopped-up things that so many places get wrong.

Testing took a while: There was an early rendition with sweet potatoes I was first excited about and later disappointed in. Later on there was tweaking of the sauce to make sure it was sharp and not just mall-gloopy. Eventually there was a mixed-veg version that didn't quite make the cut, but the celeries in it showed well. That's how we settled on this mix of celery root and plain celery—and the resulting dish was met with much approval, particularly by a beloved vegan babysitter of mine.

It was good, I thought, but was it good *enough*? I was ready to take us through another round of testing when I reached for the previous night's leftovers for breakfast and had my eureka moment: I like this dish so much more cold! Everybody else thinks I'm crazy, so go ahead and eat it hot with friends/family/strangers at the hostel, but save a smidge for the morning with your coffee.

**MAKES 4 SERVINGS**

## SAUCE

| | |
|---|---|
| **1 T** | Chinkiang vinegar |
| **1 T** | Shaoxing wine or sherry |
| **1 T** | soy sauce |
| **1 t** | sesame oil |
| **1 t** | sugar |
| **1 t** | cornstarch |

## STIR-FRY

| | |
|---|---|
| **2 T** | neutral oil |
| **1** | medium celery root (about 1½ lb), peeled and cut into ½" dice |
| **+** | kosher salt |
| **2** | celery stalks, cut into ½" pieces |
| **1** | red bell pepper, cut into ½" pieces |
| **5** | scallions, white and green parts separated, thinly sliced |
| **1** | jalapeño chili, sliced (2 T) |
| **1 T** | chopped garlic (2 to 3 cloves) |
| **1 T** | chopped fresh ginger (about 1") |
| **10** | dried Tianjin chilies or chiles de árbol, or 1 t chili flakes |
| **1 t** | cracked Sichuan peppercorns |
| **2 T** | chili oil |
| **¼ C** | roasted peanuts |

**1** Make the sauce: Stir together the vinegar, wine, soy sauce, sesame oil, sugar, cornstarch, and 2 tablespoons water in a small bowl to dissolve the sugar and cornstarch. Set aside.

**2** For the stir-fry: Heat 1 tablespoon of the neutral oil in a wok or large skillet over medium-high heat. After a minute, add the celery root, toss to coat in oil, and cook until lightly browned in spots and steaming hot, about 3 minutes. Season with salt, toss again, and add ¼ cup water to the pan. Cover, reduce the heat to medium-low, and steam the celery root until nearly tender, about 10 minutes. Transfer to a plate with a slotted spoon. Wipe out the wok (you're not cleaning it, you're just getting rid of any bits that will burn when the fire comes back) and return it to the heat.

**3** Heat the remaining 1 tablespoon oil in the wok over high heat. Add the celery and bell pepper and stir-fry for 1 minute. Add the scallion whites, jalapeño, garlic, and ginger and stir-fry for 30 seconds. Add the dried chilies and peppercorns and stir-fry for 10 seconds. Return the celery root to the wok and toss to combine everything. Pour in the reserved sauce and toss to coat all. Bring the mixture to a full boil. Once the sauce thickens, remove the pan from the heat, stir in the chili oil, and sprinkle with peanuts and scallion greens. Serve hot with rice. Or cold with coffee.

MAINLY
POTATOES

# TURNIPS, GARLIC, AND ANCHOVIES

I don't want to say I was prejudiced against turnips before trying them this way, but I know that admitting my faults is the first step to recovery. I was okay with the picturesque and comparably mild hakurei turnips, raw and cooked, probably because I played enough Super Mario Bros. as a child that they were subconsciously imprinted on me. The thought of this side dish, prepared one New Year's Eve to go with a roast of pork, terrified me. It sounded like sad wet pig food from the British countryside (boiled turnips, a hulking variety of no particular distinction) in Riviera drag (the garlic, anchovies, and parsley). The results were good enough that they converted me to turnip fandom immediately and I left the perfectly roasted pig more or less untouched as I went back for seconds and thirds of the tubers!

**MAKES 8 SERVINGS**

| | |
|---|---|
| **18** | garlic cloves, unpeeled |
| **1** | tin (2 oz) flat anchovy fillets, drained and finely chopped (about 12 fillets) |
| **1 T** | capers, rinsed |
| **½ C** | chopped curly parsley |
| **2 T** | extra-virgin olive oil |
| **1 T** | red wine vinegar |
| **+** | freshly ground black pepper |
| **+** | kosher salt |
| **2 lb** | turnips, peeled and chopped into bite-size-plus pieces |
| **+** | turnip greens reserved, chopped, if available (or, though this is very optional, substitute 2 C arugula) |

**1** Heat the oven to 300°F or 350°F.

**2** Separate the cloves of garlic but keep them in their paper jackets. Arrange them on a baking sheet and roast them until they turn a goldenish brown and are custardy soft, about 30 minutes. Squeeze them out of their skins and mash them in a small bowl.

**3** Add the anchovies, capers, parsley, oil, vinegar, and pepper to the bowl with the mashed garlic and keep the dressing at the ready.

**4** Put a pot of water on to boil and salt it well. Drop your turnips in the boiling salted water and boil them for 15 minutes. (You can test by scooting a sample piece out of the pot onto a cutting board where it should offer no meaningful resistance to a sharp knife—but should not be ready to fall to shambles either.) When the turnips are cooked to your liking, add the greens to the boiling water, then drain the contents of the pot straight away. Transfer to a serving bowl, add the dressing, and toss until completely coated. Serve hot!

# HASSELBACK POTATOES

Hasselbacks are a variation on the baked potato that go in and out of vogue every half-dozen years. Their appeal is easy to understand: They have all the rich and satisfying attributes of a baked potato plus the crispiness of a potato chip or pan-fried potato.

The waxing and waning of their popularity is probably tied to what it takes to make them: It is significantly more preparation and work than a baked potato requires, which is right next to none. Still, it's not at all difficult, and if you're at all inclined to have a luxury baked-potato experience, you will be pleased with the results.

For the trivia nerds: These potatoes picked up their name in 1953, when they were devised by a cook at the Hasselbacken Hotel in Stockholm, where they are still served today.

**MAKES 4 SERVINGS**

| | |
|---|---|
| **4** | russet potatoes |
| ¼ **C** | olive oil |
| **+** | kosher salt |
| **4 T** | unsalted butter |
| **+** | Maldon sea salt |

**1** Heat the oven to 400°F.

**2** Peel the potatoes, if you like. Shave or cut a thin slice off of one long side of each potato, creating a flat bottom so they won't roll while you prepare them. Set one potato between two chopsticks and slice the potatoes crosswise at ⅛-inch intervals, stopping at the chopstick so that you don't cut through the potato.

**3** Fill a large bowl with cold water and add the potatoes. While they are submerged, fan the layers out, using the water to rinse the starch from between the layers—this will help you achieve crispness later on. Remove the potatoes from the water and shake dry. Wrap each in a paper (or kitchen) towel and drain, cut side down, for 5 minutes.

**4** Unwrap the potatoes and place them in a wide bowl. Dress them with the olive oil, making sure to oil in between the cuts. Who knew you'd grow up to become a potato masseuse? You're doing a great job.

**5** Set the potatoes in a cast iron or other similarly hefty ovenproof skillet and drizzle them with the oil from the bowl. Sprinkle with kosher salt and transfer the skillet to the oven. Roast, basting the potatoes with the olive oil every 20 minutes, until the potatoes are tender in the center and golden on the outside, 1 hour to 1 hour 15 minutes.

**6** Use something heatproof to sheathe the handle of the skillet and bring it up to the stovetop. Dial the burner up to medium and add the butter to the pan. Baste the potatoes with the sizzling fat every 30 or so seconds for about 5 minutes, until they are irresistibly crisp and golden. Drain them on paper towels and shower them with Maldon salt. Serve hot. (A little pile of caramelized onions wouldn't hurt at this moment, and neither would an austere red wine looking for a friend to help it loosen up.)

# LATKES

I know couples who fight over what style of latke is best and/or right. Since I grew up outside of the latke-making-and-eating tradition (I am ashamed of my Irish ancestors for not figuring them out), my relationship to potato pancakes is not freighted with my-mom-did-it-this-way baggage. Instead, when I moved to New York I happened into a friendship with a man named Mitchell Davis who had just published a cookbook called *The Mensch Chef,* which describes him perfectly. Mitchell's latkes were the first latkes I ever loved and cooked, and are, to my mind, not just the greatest latkes but the *only* latkes. They are crisp, not cakey or "tender" or whatever the worst kind of latkes are. They use a two-to-one ratio of potatoes to onions, which is excellent for the aforementioned crispness and also for deliciousness. They call for matzo meal, not flour, because matzo meal > flour. In lieu of matzo meal I might crush up saltines and dial down the salt in the mixture, but a box of matzo meal is so cheap it's hard to justify not keeping one around.

**MAKES TWENTY-FOUR 4-INCH PANCAKES**

- **2 lb** russet potatoes
- **1 lb** yellow onions
- **2** eggs, beaten
- **¼ C** matzo meal or crushed saltine crackers
- **2 t** kosher salt, plus more for finishing
- **¼ t** freshly ground black pepper
- **+** neutral oil, for frying
- **+** for serving: sour cream, applesauce, ketchup

**1** Peel the potatoes and onions and grate them with a box grater—set it inside a dish and grate the potatoes lengthwise into long strands. Grate the onions over the potatoes and toss them with your hands to combine. (The onion juice will keep the potatoes from turning brown.)

**2** Place the potato-and-onion mixture into a clean kitchen towel, gather the corners, and squeeze the bundle to expel as much liquid as possible. Dump the mixture into a large bowl and add the eggs, matzo meal, salt, and pepper. Mix with a fork or your hands until the mixture is uniform.

**3** Pour ⅛ inch oil into a 12-inch skillet (that should be about ¾ cup) and heat over medium heat. Drop a few strands of potato into the oil as your canaries in the coal mine: Once they sizzle, the oil is ready for latke making. Using three fingers, loosely pick up ⅓ to ½ cup of latke mixture and lay it into the oil, forming a 3- to 4-inch round with plenty of loose strands around the edges. Repeat to form 4 pancakes.

**4** Cook the latkes until the bottoms are golden brown and crispy, 6 to 8 minutes. Flip them with a slotted spatula (I could imagine Mitchell using a Peltex, one of those fish spatulas that were once all the rage with pro chefs) and continue frying, moderating the heat so they cook evenly and do not burn, until crispy all over, another 6 to 7 minutes. Remove them with a slotted spatula and lay on a baking sheet lined with paper towels. Pour enough oil to measure ⅛ inch again and continue cooking latkes.

**5** If the latkes become cold before serving, reheat in a warm oven until crispy, 5 to 10 minutes (don't hold them in the oven or they will dry out). Salt lightly before serving. Serve hot with sour cream, applesauce, and ketchup. (My preference is yellow mustard, but I think that's wrong to do to a latke!)

# JERUSALEM ARTICHOKES WITH KETCHUP

Here are some truths:

1. Joe Beef, in Montreal, is one of the world's greatest restaurants, but not in some assholey world's-greatest-restaurant way. It manages to be epic and humble at the same time.

2. Jerusalem artichokes get a bad rap. This is largely a prejudice we inherited from Europe, where they are regarded as fart-inducing pig food that should only be eaten during wartime.

3. Ketchup is good with everything.

Here's how those truths fit together: Fred Morin and Dave McMillan, the guys behind Joe Beef, both worked for Normand Laprise, who is like the Paul Bocuse of Montreal. This is the way Laprise cooked Jerusalem artichokes, which is therefore how Fred and Dave learned to do it. And it was good enough for them to put on the menu at Joe Beef, which means that this is how you make a vegetable with a wrinkled reputation stand tall. The ketchup just sweetens the deal.

**MAKES 4 SERVINGS**

| | |
|---|---|
| **2 T** | unsalted butter or olive oil |
| **8** | large Jerusalem artichokes (about 1 lb) |
| **¼ C** | water |
| **+** | big handful of coarse or kosher salt |
| **+** | pretzel salt (or another large finishing salt like Maldon) |
| **+** | freshly ground black pepper |
| **+** | leaves from 3 thyme sprigs |
| **+** | ketchup, for serving |

**1** Heat the oven to 400°F. Smear the butter onto a nonstick rimmed baking sheet or cast iron pan.

**2** The Joe Beef secret for cleaning Jerusalem artichokes: Put your artichokes in a large, heavy-duty zip-top plastic bag and pour in the water. Add the coarse salt, seal the bag, and shake the bag vigorously. Athletically. Now open the bag and rinse the artichokes well. You're getting all the dirt and debris off better than your hands would.

**3** Halve the damp artichokes lengthwise and arrange them, cut side down, in a single layer on the prepared pan. Season them generously with the pretzel salt and a little pepper. Strew the thyme leaves evenly over the top.

**4** Place in the oven and roast for 40 minutes. Turn the artichokes over and roast until browned and slightly shriveled, another 15 to 30 minutes. Serve them warm, with plenty of ketchup.

# SYRACUSE SALT POTATOES

We are not so many pages removed from my buddy Dave Chang saying that a recipe with two ingredients is not a power vegetable. I beg to differ, at least in this case. I remember the first time I had these at our friends' commune in upstate New York. Potatoes boiled in salted water didn't sound like it could be anything more than what it is, but I didn't adjust my expectations for the perverse amount at play—basically a 4:1 ratio of salt to water. This salinity makes the water boil at a higher temperature than water usually does, and while I can't explain the chemistry of why that's good, I can tell you it more or less "bakes" the potatoes, leaving a crust of crystallized salt on the skin and a surprisingly creamy, not-very-salty center inside. They go with everything you eat and cook during the summer, from corn to hot dogs and back again.

**MAKES 4 SERVINGS**

| | |
|---|---|
| **10 oz** | kosher salt (about 2 C) |
| **8 C** | water |
| **2 lb** | new potatoes |
| **4 T** | unsalted butter, melted |

**1** Combine the salt with the water in a large pot. Cover and bring to a boil. The temperature will be between 218°F and 222°F.

**2** Add the potatoes and return to a boil. Cook until the potatoes are tender, about 25 minutes. Drain and place the potatoes in a serving dish. As they dry, crystallized salt will appear on the skins. This is good.

**3** Serve the potatoes hot, with the melted butter alongside for dunking.

# MCALOO TIKKI™ SANDWICH

The McAloo Tikki is the *Power Vegetables!* veggie burger. They are burgers that are crisp in a way that meat never is or should be, and an amalgam of textures and flavors that would make whoever invented the Whopper proud.

**MAKES 4 SANDWICHES**

| | |
|---|---|
| **2** | garlic cloves |
| **1** | serrano or jalapeño chili |
| **1** | piece (1") fresh ginger |
| **2 t** | coriander seeds |
| **2 t** | cumin seeds |
| **1 t** | ground turmeric |
| **1 t** | kosher salt |
| **½ C** | fresh or frozen peas |
| **3 T** | mayonnaise |
| **1 T** | ketchup |
| **+** | thinly sliced red onion |
| **+** | thinly sliced beefsteak tomato |
| **1 C** | loosely packed cilantro leaves |
| **4** | potato hamburger buns |
| **1** | large russet potato, peeled (about 12 oz) |
| **+** | neutral oil, for frying |

**1** Finely grate the garlic, chili, and ginger into a large bowl. There should be about 1 tablespoon of each. Add the spices—coriander seeds, cumin seeds, turmeric, and salt—and the peas to the bowl. Set aside.

**2** Set up your assembly line: Stir the mayo and ketchup together in a small bowl to make the special sauce. Arrange the rings of red onion and tomatoes on a plate. Have your cilantro and buns ready and waiting.

**3** When ready to cook, set a box grater in a shallow bowl or pie plate and grate the potato into the receptacle. Use your hands or a kitchen towel to squeeze the liquid from the potato. You aren't looking to wring it dry, just to extract what's there to be extracted. Toss the squeezed potato into the bowl with the seasonings and use your hands to fold and mix.

**4** Pour ¼ inch of oil into a 12-inch skillet, preferably cast iron, and heat over medium heat. Eyeball the potato mixture into 4 portions in the bowl and use a gentle grasp to lift one portion from the bowl and deposit it as a lacy-edged mound in one quadrant of the pan. Repeat with the remaining portions to form four lacy potato-pea mounds. Fry the McAloo patties without moving or pressing on them for 3 minutes. When the edges have become golden brown, use a slotted metal spatula to release the patties from the bottom of the pan and carefully flip them so as not to splash any hot oil on you or your friends. Cook the McAloo on the second side until crispy, then re-flip and cook until the whole thing is mahogany brown and quite crunchy all over. Transfer to a plate lined with paper towels.

**5** Assembly-line your McAloos: Smear a bit of special sauce on each cut side of the buns. Set a patty on the bottom bun and top with a few rings of red onion, a couple slices of tomato, and a handful of cilantro leaves. Eat at once.

# BREAD & CAKE

# CARROT CAKE

Power and vegetables aside, carrot cake with cream cheese frosting rules.

|   |   |
|---|---|
| **4** | eggs |
| **2 C** | sugar |
| **1 C** | vegetable oil, plus more for the pans |
| **2 t** | ground cinnamon |
| **1 t** | kosher salt |
| **+** | pinch of ground cloves |
| **2 C** | all-purpose flour |
| **2 t** | baking soda |
| **3 C** | grated carrot |
| **½ C** | chopped crystallized ginger |
|   | Cream Cheese Frosting (recipe follows) |

**1** Heat the oven to 350°F for cake or 375°F for cupcakes. Grease a 13 × 9-inch baking pan, two 9-inch round cake pans, or line 24 cups of two standard muffin tins with paper liners.

**2** Whisk together the eggs, sugar, oil, cinnamon, salt, and ground cloves in a large bowl until smooth. Stir together the flour and baking soda in a separate small bowl, then stir them into the eggy mixture. Whisk until smooth again, about 30 seconds, then use a large spatula or spoon to fold in the carrot and ginger.

**3** Pour the batter into the greased pan(s). Bake until a toothpick inserted into the center of the cake or cupcake comes out clean, 15 to 20 minutes for cupcakes, 40 to 50 minutes for a large cake. Let cool for 10 minutes, then remove whatever you've baked from whatever it was baked in, and cool completely on a rack before frosting.

## CREAM CHEESE FROSTING

**MAKES ABOUT 2 CUPS**

|   |   |
|---|---|
| **8 oz** | cream cheese, at room temperature |
| **1** | stick (4 oz) unsalted butter, at room temperature |
| **+** | pinch of salt |
| **4 C** | powdered sugar |
| **1 t** | vanilla extract |

Combine the cream cheese, butter, and salt in a stand mixer or a large bowl and whip together until smooth and fluffy, about 2 minutes. Stop the machine, scrape down the sides, and add 1 cup of the powdered sugar. Start it on low, then increase speed, whipping to completely incorporate the sugar. Continue this process until all the sugar is incorporated. Finally add the vanilla and whip an additional 10 seconds. Hold the frosting at room temperature until you're ready to frost your cake(s).

# POTATO ROSEMARY BREAD

This is an idiotproof loaf of fantastic flavor and moisture that lasts for a few days. It harnesses the power of potatoes in a way that deeply warms my mostly Irish heart. Say hello to your new favorite home-baked loaf.

■■ ■■ ■■■ ■■■■

**MAKES TWO 8-INCH LOAVES**

## STARTER

| | |
|---|---|
| ¼ C | bread flour |
| 2 T | water |
| + | pinch of fresh yeast |

## BREAD DOUGH

| | |
|---|---|
| 2 | medium russet potatoes (about 1 lb) |
| 3½ C | bread flour, plus more for dusting |
| 1 C + 1 T | water |
| 4 t | kosher salt |
| 2 t | fresh yeast, or 1 t active dry yeast |
| 2 T | olive oil, plus more for greasing |
| 2 T | chopped garlic |
| 2 t | chopped fresh rosemary |

**1** Make the starter: Stir together the flour, water, and yeast in a small bowl until smooth. Cover with plastic wrap and let the starter sit in a warmish spot for 12 hours.

**2** Make the bread dough: Heat the oven to 350°F. Prick each potato a dozen times with a fork and bake until tender, about 1 hour. Remove and when cool enough to handle, halve the potatoes, scoop out the cooked flesh, and coarsely mash it with a fork.

**3** In the bowl of a stand mixer fitted with a dough hook, mix the flour and water to form a dry, shaggy dough. Stop the mixer and let the dough stand for 15 minutes. If you're making the dough by hand, simply stir together the flour and water with a wooden spoon until combined, then let stand 15 minutes. (For the nerds at home, this stage is called autolysis, and it means you're giving the enzymes that are in your flour a chance to get started on the work of breaking down the proteins and starches they're hanging out with, and it makes the dough easier to handle.)

**4** Add the starter, salt, and yeast and mix at low speed until fully combined, about 5 minutes. Increase the speed to medium and knead until the dough is smooth and supple, about 10 minutes. (If you're doing this by hand, wet your hands as you knead it if the dough becomes very stiff.) Pull off a 1-inch ball of dough and stretch it thinly between your pointer fingers and thumbs to form a rectangle. If it becomes thin enough to see light through it before it tears, the dough is ready. Add the potatoes, olive oil, rosemary, and garlic, and knead on low speed until they are incorporated

*recipe continues*

into the dough. (Working by hand, cut the dough into a half-dozen pieces and dump into a bowl with the potatoes, olive oil, and rosemary. With two hands, knead and wrestle with the ingredients until they become one, about 4 minutes. Shape into a ball.)

**5** Transfer the dough to an oiled bowl, turn to coat it with the oil, cover the bowl with plastic wrap, and let rise at room temperature for 1 hour.

**6** Working in the bowl, grab the dough on a far edge and fold it in toward the middle, deflating it a bit. Rotate the bowl 180 degrees and fold the far edge of the dough toward the middle. Turn 90 degrees and fold, turn another 90 degrees and fold. Turn over the dough ball so the seam side is down, cover it with plastic, and let rise for 1 hour.

**7** Very lightly flour a large work surface. Scrape the dough out onto the floured surface and divide into two equal pieces. Cover with plastic and let rest for 15 minutes. Working with one piece at a time, on that floured surface, gently press the dough to flatten it and release the gas trapped within it. Turn the edges under the center of the dough, forming a smooth round ball or other bread-like shape. Repeat with the remaining dough to form two round loaves.

**8** Lay a linen kitchen towel on a baking sheet and flour it generously. Set one loaf on either end of the towel. Gather the center of the towel by the edges and lift it up to form a pleat between the two loaves. Cover loosely with plastic wrap and proof for 1 hour.

**9** While the bread proofs, place a large pizza stone, cast iron griddle, or 2 large Dutch ovens with lids on the middle rack of the oven and heat to 450°F. If using a pizza stone or griddle, place a rimmed baking sheet on the rack below.

**10** Working quickly, uncover the loaves and slash them a few times with a sharp knife (or a razor blade if you're the sort of person who keeps those around the house). Immediately transfer the loaves to the stone or griddle and add 2 cups of ice to the rimmed baking sheet below, and close the oven door. (This will create steam, which ensures a crusty loaf.) If using Dutch ovens, place the dough inside and cover with a lid. (The bread will create its own steam.) Resist the urge to open the oven door or remove the lids, lest the steam escape. Bake for 40 minutes, until the bread is dark brown, crisp, and sounds hollow when tapped on the bottom. Cool completely before slicing.

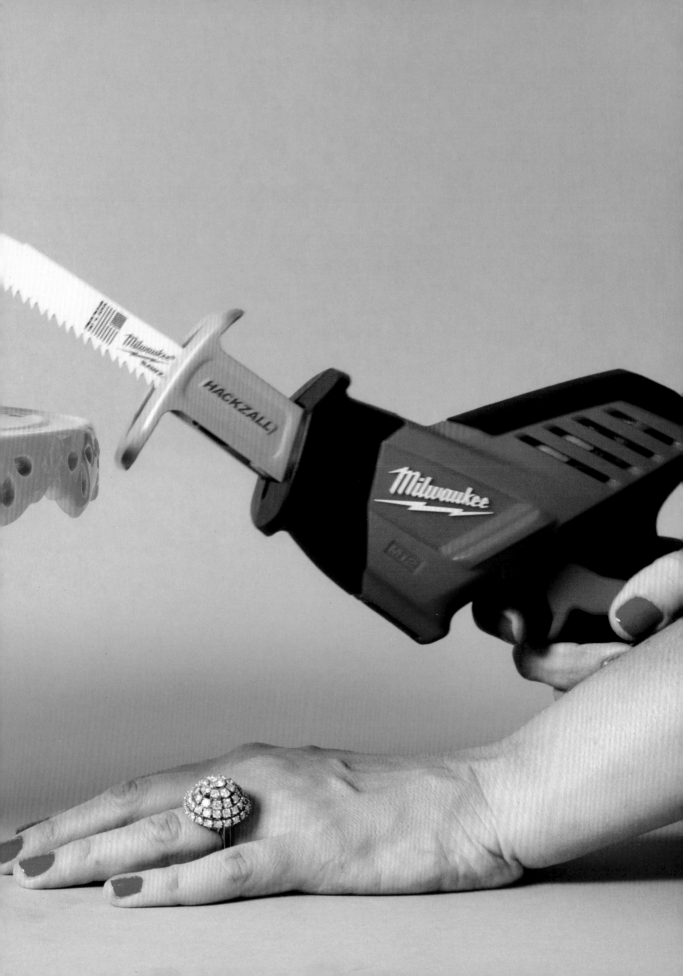

# ZUCCHINI BREAD

Like banana bread, but made with zucchini, which is like a vegetable, except it's actually a fruit. It's okay, don't think too hard about it: Just embrace the power.

This zucchini bread is awesome because it is dense and slices like date bread or something else healthy and full of moisture and fiber. Slather it with soft, salted butter or whipped cream cheese. It is equally delicious in the summer—made from the oversize monster zucchini that show up after it rains—as it is around the holidays. It makes two loaves and freezes beautifully wrapped in plastic wrap and foil.

**MAKES 2 LOAVES**

| | |
|---|---|
| **1 C** | neutral oil, plus more for the pans |
| **3** | eggs |
| **2 C** | sugar |
| **1 T** | vanilla extract |
| **2 C** | all-purpose flour |
| **2 t** | baking soda |
| **½ t** | baking powder |
| **1 T** | ground cinnamon |
| **1 t** | kosher salt |
| **2 C** | grated zucchini |
| **1 C** | chopped walnuts |

**1** Heat the oven to 350°F. Grease and flour two loaf pans. (If that's too bakery shorthand for you, lemme help: Rub the loaf pans with a bare slick of oil, then dust that oil with flour. It's like an edible nonstick coating for your cake-breads.)

**2** Whisk together the oil, eggs, and sugar in a bowl until the sugar dissolves. Stir in the vanilla, flour, baking soda, baking powder, cinnamon, and salt until the mixture is smooth. Fold in the zucchini and walnuts. Divide the batter between the loaf pans, smoothing the tops.

**3** Bake the loaves until a toothpick inserted into their centers comes out clean, about 55 minutes. Cool the breads in the pans on a rack for 10 minutes, then remove them from the pans to cool completely before slicing.

# PARSNIP CAKE

I do not know if my considerable fondness for this cake stems from the quantity of parsnips hidden within it or because those parsnips have been subsumed into a greater whole, a toothsome cake with an appealing but hard-to-pinpoint flavor. Regardless, it's a winner. I like it best with the Cream Cheese Frosting (page 250) but, then again, I like everything better with cream cheese frosting.

**MAKES 16 SERVINGS**

## BLOOD ORANGE BUTTERCREAM

| | |
|---|---|
| **2** | blood oranges, juiced (about ½ C juice) |
| **2** | sticks (8 oz) butter, at room temperature |
| **4 C** | powdered sugar |

## PARSNIP CAKE

| | |
|---|---|
| **3** | eggs |
| **1 C** | sugar |
| **½ C** | neutral oil |
| **½ C** | milk |
| **1 t** | kosher salt |
| **½ t** | vanilla extract |
| **1½ C** | all-purpose flour |
| **2 t** | baking powder |
| **1 t** | ground cinnamon |
| **¼ t** | grated nutmeg |
| **¼ t** | ground allspice |
| **¼ t** | ground cloves |
| **2 C** | grated parsnips (from 1 lb peeled parsnips) |
| **1 t** | grated fresh ginger or ½ t ground ginger |

**1** Make the buttercream: Pour the blood orange juice into a small saucepan and bring to a boil. Cook until reduced by half and syrupy, about 10 minutes. Remove from the heat and let cool completely.

**2** In a stand mixer fitted with the paddle attachment, cream the butter on medium-high until fluffy, about 2 minutes. Stop the machine, add the reduced blood orange juice, and beat to incorporate. Incorporate the powdered sugar into the creamed butter 1 cup at a time—stop the machine, add it, slowly stir it in, increase the speed to really beat it, then stop and repeat. This is not a don't-overwork-it thing, this is a keep-your-kitchen-from-looking-like-a-wig-powdering-room thing.

**3** Make the cake: Heat the oven to 350°F for cake or 375°F for cupcakes. Grease a 13 × 9-inch pan, two 9-inch round cake pans, or line 18 cups of a muffin tin with paper liners.

**4** Whisk together the eggs, granulated sugar, oil, milk, salt, and vanilla in a large bowl until smooth. Stir in the flour, baking powder, cinnamon, nutmeg, allspice, and ground cloves and stir together with the whisk until smooth and homogenous, about 2 minutes. Fold the parsnips and ginger into the cake batter.

**5** Pour the batter into the greased pan(s)—this batter isn't going to grow much in the oven, so fill the cake pan(s) or cupcake liners to within a half inch of the top. Bake until a toothpick inserted into the center of the cake or cupcake comes out clean, about 24 minutes for cake, 16 minutes for cupcakes. Let cool for 10 minutes, then remove whatever you've baked from whatever it was baked in, and cool completely on a rack before frosting.

# ACKNOWLEDGMENTS

I'd like to acknowledge you for looking at this book and being like, *Heheh, did he just call the book* Power Vegetables! *so he could run out to Spencer's and buy a bunch of plasma balls? Whatever, I bet this is a book of simple vegetarian-ish recipes I'll want to make on weeknights, so I'll buy it.*

Because, yes, that is pretty much exactly the case. And now that I've acknowledged the real conceit and my true motivation for doing the book, let me indict my co-conspirators:

Hannah Clark is my wife. She's worked on all three of the *Lucky Peach* books thus far, lending her sharply critical take on what's delicious and what isn't, about what's easy and what's not, and what looks good and what doesn't to each. She is credited as the prop stylist, and she did that, but also much more, keeping the project on track and focused when I was ready to let it list.

Joanna Sciarrino, managing editor, kept me on something like a schedule, or as much of a schedule as I can be kept on. Rica Allannic, who has edited almost all the books I've done since 2009, decided to take a different tack on this one and be gentle and understanding about my ability to work in an orderly fashion; her patience for me was as welcome as it was disorienting.

Mary-Frances Heck developed these recipes from ideas into things you can cook or from chef's books into *LP* recipe-speak. As a fellow Irishperson she shares at least half the blame for the potato chapter in this book. JJ Basil and Sam Henderson both helped out with recipe development and ideas behind the scenes, and made the book better by doing so.

Gabriele Stabile and Mark Ibold were the camera and hands, respectively, of this book again, and I've run out of interesting ways to thank them. Guys: I'm surprised we don't all hate each other yet.

Brette Warshaw and other nerds at *Lucky Peach* helped out by reading this thing and weeding it for errors, which if they are still there are the fault of my lazy word-gardening. I would also like to perform an indelicately loud and demonstrative golf clap for the staff of the magazine and website, who picked up my slack whenever I was slacking off to work on this book.

The book was designed by Devin Washburn, who took to cookbook making like an IROC-Z takes to the open road. Rob Engvall made real nice drawings for it like the responsible and mature man he is, a man who would never respond to a nickname like "Bubbles" if someone directed it at him in the office. Marysarah Quinn tightened things up at the end like one of those mechanics in one of those car racing sports on TV: She did a great and essential job with no fuss and little praise so that a guy with a mustache and Oakleys could speed across the finish line, looking like it's the easiest thing in the world, and then spray himself down with champagne. (I am the guy with the mustache in this analogy.)

This book owes a debt of gratitude to the chefs who took the time to speak with me and to those whose dishes or published recipes inspired what is between these covers. Ivan Orkin, who is best known for his chicken soup, contributed two of the best recipes in here; Jessica Koslow, David Chang, Brooks Headley, and Julia Goldberg all helped us narrow the scope and focus the mission of the book. There were also plenty of moms and normals who helped build the book up, with the biggest debt owed to Ritu Krishna, who contributed three recipes to this volume.

My brothers and sisters at the commune contributed to the way I thought about vegetables and every-night deliciousness; Katherine and Bradley and Chloe and the Hoopers are influencers all.

Thanks, too, to the team at Clarkson Potter: Christine Tanigawa and Derek Gullino for saving me and us from a million dumb mistakes; the incomparably mustachioed Kevin Sweeting; Natasha Martin and Kate Tyler for making sure people know the books exist; and Doris Cooper and Aaron Wehner for their ongoing belief in and support of my harebrained schemes.

Here are a few name-only shout-outs to dudes who contributed in different ways: Steve Kent, Walter Green, Jason Polan, Tony Kim, Chris Ying. And lastly but not leastly, thanks to Kim Witherspoon and David Chang, with whom I have been entangled in many book projects and whom I hope to stay entangled with for years to come.

**pfm, 2016**

# INDEX

# CONVERSION CHART
## Equivalent Imperial and Metric Measurements

American cooks use standard containers, the 8-ounce cup and a tablespoon that takes exactly 16 level fillings to fill that cup level. Measuring by cup makes it very difficult to give weight equivalents, as a cup of densely packed butter will weigh considerably more than a cup of flour. The easiest way therefore to deal with cup measurements in recipes is to take the amount by volume rather than by weight. Thus the equation reads:

1 cup = 240 ml = 8 fl. oz.
½ cup = 120 ml = 4 fl. oz.

It is possible to buy a set of American cup measures in major stores around the world.

In the States, butter is often measured in sticks. One stick is the equivalent of 8 tablespoons. One tablespoon of butter is therefore the equivalent of ½ ounce / 15 grams.

## LIQUID MEASURES

| Fluid Ounces | U.S. | Imperial | Milliliters |
|---|---|---|---|
| | 1 teaspoon | 1 teaspoon | 5 |
| ¼ | 2 teaspoons | 1 dessertspoon | 10 |
| ½ | 1 tablespoon | 1 tablespoon | 14 |
| 1 | 2 tablespoons | 2 tablespoons | 28 |
| 2 | ¼ cup | 4 tablespoons | 56 |
| 4 | ½ cup | | 120 |
| 5 | | ¼ pint or 1 gill | 140 |
| 6 | ¾ cup | | 170 |
| 8 | 1 cup | | 240 |
| 9 | | | 250, ¼ liter |
| 10 | 1¼ cups | ½ pint | 280 |
| 12 | 1½ cups | | 340 |
| 15 | | ¾ pint | 420 |
| 16 | 2 cups | | 450 |
| 18 | 2¼ cups | | 500, ½ liter |
| 20 | 2½ cups | 1 pint | 560 |
| 24 | 3 cups | | 675 |
| 25 | | 1¼ pints | 700 |
| 27 | 3½ cups | | 750 |
| 30 | 3¾ cups | 1½ pints | 840 |
| 32 | 4 cups or 1 quart | | 900 |
| 35 | | 1¾ pints | 980 |
| 36 | 4½ cups | | 1000, 1 liter |
| 40 | 5 cups | 2 pints or 1 quart | 1120 |

## SOLID MEASURES

| U.S. and Imperial Measures | | Metric Measures | |
|---|---|---|---|
| Ounces | Pounds | Grams | Kilos |
| 1 | | 28 | |
| 2 | | 56 | |
| 3½ | | 100 | |
| 4 | ¼ | 112 | |
| 5 | | 140 | |
| 6 | | 168 | |
| 8 | ½ | 225 | |
| 9 | | 250 | ¼ |
| 12 | ¾ | 340 | |
| 16 | 1 | 450 | |
| 18 | | 500 | ½ |
| 20 | 1¼ | 560 | |
| 24 | 1½ | 675 | |
| 27 | | 750 | ¾ |
| 28 | 1¾ | 780 | |
| 32 | 2 | 900 | |
| 36 | 2¼ | 1000 | 1 |
| 40 | 2½ | 1100 | |
| 48 | 3 | 1350 | |
| 54 | | 1500 | 1½ |

## OVEN TEMPERATURE EQUIVALENTS

| Fahrenheit | Celsius | Gas Mark | Description |
|---|---|---|---|
| 225 | 110 | ¼ | Cool |
| 250 | 130 | ½ | |
| 275 | 140 | 1 | Very Slow |
| 300 | 150 | 2 | |
| 325 | 170 | 3 | Slow |
| 350 | 180 | 4 | Moderate |
| 375 | 190 | 5 | |
| 400 | 200 | 6 | Moderately Hot |
| 425 | 220 | 7 | Fairly Hot |
| 450 | 230 | 8 | Hot |
| 475 | 240 | 9 | Very Hot |
| 500 | 250 | 10 | Extremely Hot |

Any broiling recipes can be used with the grill of the oven, but beware of high-temperature grills.

**LUCKY PEACH** is an award-winning independent food magazine that publishes daily on luckypeach.com and quarterly as a printed journal. *Lucky Peach* has authored two previous books with Clarkson Potter: *Lucky Peach Presents 101 Easy Asian Recipes* and *The Wurst of Lucky Peach.*

**PETER MEEHAN** is the editor and cofounder of *Lucky Peach*. A former columnist for the *New York Times*, he is also the coauthor of numerous cookbooks, including the *New York Times* bestselling *Momofuku* and *The Frankies Spuntino Kitchen Companion and Cooking Manual*. He lives in New York.

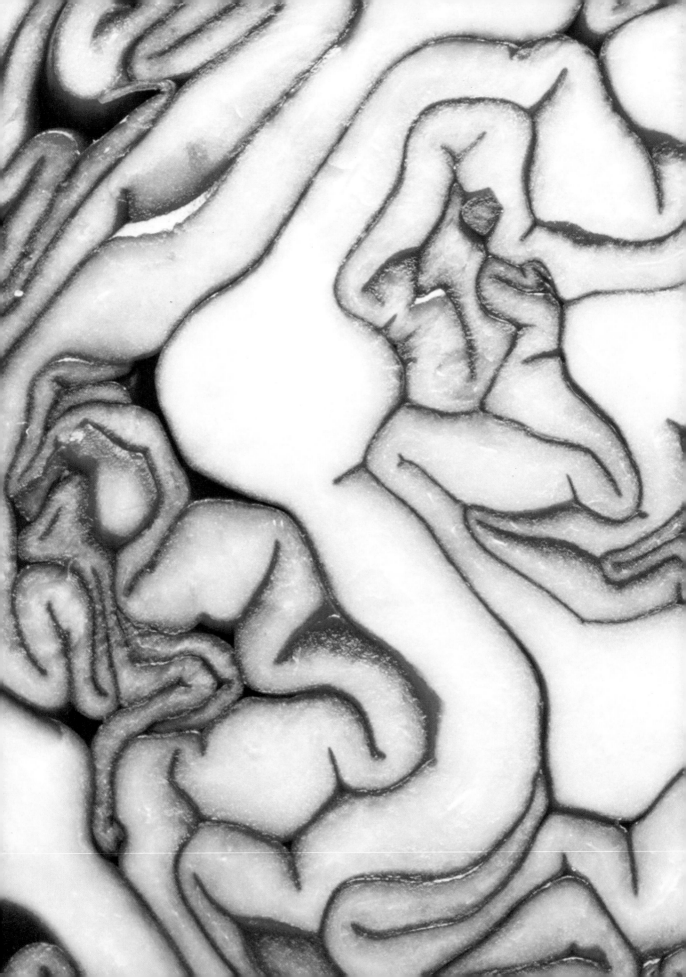